FIRST
FOODS

THIRD EDITION

FIRST
FOODS

THIRD EDITION

GLENCOE

Macmillan/McGraw-Hill

Lake Forest, Illinois
Columbus, Ohio
Mission Hills, California
Peoria, Illinois

Roberta Larson Duyff

Marion L. Cronan

June C. Atwood

Send all inquiries to:
Glencoe Division, Macmillan/McGraw-Hill
809 West Detweiller Drive
Peoria, IL 61615-2190

ISBN 0-02-672330-1

5 6 7 8 9 10 11 12 13 14 15   99 98 97 96 95 94 93 92 91 90

Book Design By: William Seabright

PREFACE

FIRST FOODS is an introduction to food experiences through easy steps, using many convenience foods.

Each chapter will help you to know more about the foods you experience daily. Preparing and serving food creatively is fun, especially when the results please you, your family, and your friends.

Children, teenagers, and adults alike entertain at home with food. In this book you will find ideas for breakfast, brunches, lunches, light meals, and fancy dinners, as well as special occasions.

Throughout this text you will read about nutrition and learn how to apply that knowledge in developing healthy food habits. You will learn how individuals can control their weight and maintain their good health. Knowing how to choose a nutritious diet is so important to your health that throughout the book hints are given to help you.

This book is full of many practical suggestions, such as being a wise consumer, packing a lunch for school, or eating out. These suggestions can be put to use at once.

Each chapter is organized for easy learning beginning with objectives that tell you what the chapter is about and the new vocabulary words—defined for easy reference. Throughout the chapter, the vocabulary words are high-lighted and defined. Illustrations reinforce the content to make it easy to understand. Lab activities within the chapter provide in-school or at-home food experiences directly related to the chapter topic.

Throughout the text you will find many tips for working efficiently with your kitchen group at school. These tips will help you get good results in a short time.

At the end of each chapter, you will find a summary which states the important concepts, review questions, and suggested activities to reinforce the content—all designed to make learning about foods and nutrition exciting and fun!

CONTENTS

FOOD AND YOU

aroma	the way food smells
appetite	the desire to eat
emotions	the way you feel about things
ethnic foods	foods from people of various parts of the world
food habits	the type of foods you eat, when you eat, and how you eat
lifestyle	the way you live
regional foods	foods popular in a particular part of the country
snacks	foods eaten between meals
taste buds	parts of the tongue that identify different tastes
wellness	being totally healthy in mind, body, and emotions

After reading this chapter, you should be able to:

- *explain four reasons why people eat.*
- *name at least five things that affect what foods people eat.*
- *explain how lifestyles affect meals and snacks.*
- *list places where people eat.*

W hat do you think of when you hear the word, "food"? Perhaps it makes you hungry. Or your favorite foods come to mind. Maybe you think of cooking or being healthy. The word, "food," just might make you smile!

Food means many different things to different people. The way you think about food is shown in your food habits. *Food habits* include the types of food you eat, when you eat, and how you eat.

Where you are often determines what you eat.

Why Do You Eat?

Why do you suppose people eat? The obvious answer is "to stay alive." But people eat for other reasons, too.

Food Keeps You Well

The main reason you eat and drink is to stay alive, but food gives you energy, too, and helps you grow. Beyond that, food helps keep you well. *Wellness* means being totally healthy. That includes your body, mind, and emotions. *Emotions* are your feelings about things.

When you're healthy, you have pep or lots of energy. You're alert and ready to learn. You look your best. And you feel good about yourself. In this book, you'll learn to choose foods that help keep you well.

Food Tastes Good!

Suppose a piping hot pizza is set in front of you. It has all your favorite toppings! Why would you eat it? Most people would say, "It looks good. It smells good. And I know it will taste good!"

How does your brain know how food tastes? First, you feast with your eyes and nose. They send messages to your brain. You see and smell the pizza and then remember how good it tastes. And so you're ready to dig in!

Taste buds on your tongue can taste four things—sweet, sour, bitter, and salty. The rest of food's flavor comes from its *aroma*, or smell.

Almost everyone likes to eat! Eating is a pleasure when food looks, smells, and tastes good.

HOW'S IT TASTE?

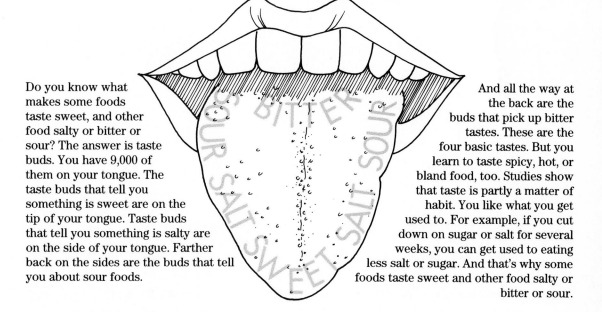

Do you know what makes some foods taste sweet, and other food salty or bitter or sour? The answer is taste buds. You have 9,000 of them on your tongue. The taste buds that tell you something is sweet are on the tip of your tongue. Taste buds that tell you something is salty are on the side of your tongue. Farther back on the sides are the buds that tell you about sour foods.

And all the way at the back are the buds that pick up bitter tastes. These are the four basic tastes. But you learn to taste spicy, hot, or bland food, too. Studies show that taste is partly a matter of habit. You like what you get used to. For example, if you cut down on sugar or salt for several weeks, you can get used to eating less salt or sugar. And that's why some foods taste sweet and other food salty or bitter or sour.

People often eat when they're bored and this can lead to being overweight. Next time you're bored and find yourself heading for the refrigerator try a change of pace instead. Go for a walk, call a friend, or rearrange your room.

Food Satisfies Your Emotions

Have you ever gone to the refrigerator when you were bored or tense? Many people eat when they're lonely, bored, upset, or tense. They think that eating makes them feel better. Eating is a way to satisfy emotions. Sometimes emotions get in the way, and people eat too much.

People eat when they're happy, too. Happiness is another emotion. Maybe they have a special meal to celebrate an award, a graduation, or turning sixteen. What might you eat if you were celebrating?

Emotions also affect your appetite. *Appetite* is your desire to eat. Some people don't feel like eating at all when they're not happy. Feeling happy, however, often goes along with a good appetite.

STORIES OF FOODS

- The **hamburger,** a typical American food, came from Hamburg, Germany, in the 1870's. It was ground beefsteak. In 1904 at the St. Louis World's Fair, hamburgers were first sold on buns.

- **Ice cream cones** were invented at the 1904 St. Louis World's Fair, too. An ice cream stand ran out of glass dishes. A salesman had a smart idea. He rolled thin waffles from a pastry stand into a cone. The cones became an ice cream "dish"!

- **Popcorn** is an American Indian food. History suggests that they brought it to the Pilgrim's Thanksgiving feast in 1621.

- **Peanut butter** was invented by an American doctor in 1890 for his patients. They needed a high-protein food.

- **Raisins** were first made as an accident! In 1873 the sun was very hot in California. Juicy grapes dried up on the vines. One clever grower didn't destroy the grapes. Instead he sold them as something special, "Peruvian delicacies." And a new food was invented.

Food Is Part of Being Together

People often eat because they're together. Sharing food is part of sharing friendship. For example, when you have friends over, you probably offer them something to eat or drink. You may eat even if you're not hungry.

Eating together is part of your upbringing. First you ate with your family. As a youngster, you probably snacked with small friends. At school, you ate meals with other students. People often eat out when they date. Adults eat with fellow workers. Throughout your life, you'll share friendship, conversation, and laughter while you eat.

Food is often a gift of friendship, too. Cookies and breads make nice holiday gifts. A fruit basket gives a warm "hello" or "get well." Homemade food is also a nice gift for a hostess.

What Influences Your Food Choices?

Does everyone in your class eat the same foods? Probably not. Food choices are very individual. Everyone eats and likes different foods. Many things affect what foods you eat and like.

Your Family

Your family first influenced your food choices. As a baby, they fed you. They chose what foods you'd eat. As you grew up, you learned to like many of the foods they liked. That's why some of your favorite foods are the same.

Your Ethnic Background

Families pass down food habits from one generation to the next. People who came to America from other countries brought their ways of cooking with them. Their children and grandchildren might still eat these foods. Foods from people who come from various parts of the world are called *ethnic foods.* The chart on page 17 shows foods which ethnic groups brought to America. Which of these foods are familiar to you?

People in the United States are lucky. We can enjoy foods of many other ethnic groups. For example, Italian, Mexican, and Chinese foods are eaten all over America!

Religion

Religion can influence what foods people eat. On religious holidays special food customs may be followed. Some teachings forbid certain foods. Muslims and many Jewish people, for example, don't eat pork. Hindus don't eat beef. According to orthodox Jewish law, meat and dairy foods can't be eaten at the same meal. Catholics give up certain foods during Lent.

FOODS WE EAT FROM OTHER COUNTRIES

Food	Place	Description
Chicken Curry	India	Chicken dish made with special spices
Egg Roll	China	Egg and vegetables wrapped in a thin pancake and fried
Fish and Chips	England	Fried fish and fried potatoes
Kiwi (KEE wee) Fruit	New Zealand	A fruit that's green on the inside with a fuzzy brown peel
Lasagna (lah ZAH nya)	Italy	Dish made with wide, flat noodles, meat, cheese, and tomato sauce
Okra (OH krah)	Africa	A green vegetable
Paella (peye AY yah)	Spain	Dish made of fish, chicken, meat, vegetables, and rice
Pita (PEE tah) Bread	Middle East	Flat, round bread with a pocket inside which is often stuffed with salad or meat
Quiche (keesh)	France	Cheese and egg pie often made with vegetables, meat, or fish
Sauerkraut (SOW er krowt)	Germany	Salted cabbage prepared in a special way
Shish Kebabs (shish KEH babz)	Middle East	Meat cut in cubes and cooked on a stick
Sushi (SOO shee)	Japan	Raw fish and rice
Tortilla (tor TEE yah)	Mexico	Round, flat bread made from corn meal or wheat flour; used to make tacos, enchiladas, and burritos

Festivals celebrate the harvest.

Special Celebrations

Food is often a large part of holiday celebrations. Many holidays wouldn't be complete without certain foods:

- cake for a birthday party
- turkey, dressing, and cranberries for Thanksgiving.
- brightly-colored eggs for Easter

Food is the main event at many get-togethers. Clambakes, fish fries, potluck dinners, and barbecues are popular in many places. Festivals, such as Dairy Days, Strawberry Festivals, and Harvest Festivals, are given to celebrate foods produced locally.

Your Friends

As you became more independent, friends began to influence your food choices. You learn to like foods popular in their families. You also introduce them to foods that are favorites in your family.

Your food choices were influenced by your friends if you've done any of these things:

- swapped sandwiches with a friend
- ordered a restaurant food just because a friend did
- tasted a new food at a friend's home

Learning about food with friends is fun. Often they teach you about new foods which can help keep you healthy. Try to teach your friends about good foods you like, too.

Some food habits you learn from friends may not be good for you. Do you know someone who always drinks soft drinks instead of milk because "everybody does it"? Milk is a much healthier food than a soft drink.

Decide what foods you need to stay healthy. Then decide if you'll follow your friends' food habits or stick to yours.

Region Where You Live

People eat foods that are popular where they live. Each region or area of the country has special foods it calls its own. These are called *regional foods*.

Different parts of the country produce certain foods in plentiful amounts. These foods become part of the area's cooking. Dishes cooked with these foods may become favorites in that region. Often when we think of that part of the country, we think of their regional food specialties. For example:

- In New England, fresh fish is served in chowders and at clambakes.
- Peaches and pecans grow well in the South. The South is known for both peach and pecan pies.

Pecans are a regional food in the south. They're not grown in other parts of the country.

The Midwest grows most of the corn produced in this country.

- The Midwest grows most of the nation's corn. Corn-on-the-cob is a summer favorite there.
- Beef is raised on ranches of the Southwest. Barbecued beef is a Southwest speciality.
- The valleys of the West grow many different fruits and vegetables. Westerners serve many creative salads.
- Pineapples come from Hawaii. Hawaiians serve pineapple with any meal.
- In Alaska, people eat bear and deer meat. Meat from wild animals is sold in the stores.

People who settled in a particular region of America also helped create the regional cooking style.

Many New England favorites started with the American Indians. The Indians taught the settlers to cook with foods from the New World. Today, New England is known for these Indian foods—turkey, succotash (lima beans and corn), cranberry sauce, and Indian pudding.

Grits, catfish, greens, okra, and hush puppies are popular in the South. These dishes combined the foods plentiful in the area with the cooking of the African and European settlers and the American Indians.

Creole cooking from Louisiana combines French, Spanish, American Indian, and African cooking styles. Gumbo, a soup made with okra, is popular there.

Many Mexicans live in the Southwest and their food customs influence the types of food eaten there. People who live there eat many Mexican foods, such as tamales, tortillas, and enchiladas.

One hundred years ago, pioneers in the West needed sourdough to make pancakes and bread. Today, sourdough bread is still common there.

Many people who live in Hawaii came from Asia. Asian foods, such as rice, Chinese vegetables, and sweet-sour pork, are also part of Hawaiian cooking.

Season of the Year

The foods you eat are the foods you can buy or grow. The season of the year often affects what you can buy and what you can eat. In summer, you usually can't buy cranberries or eggnog. Those foods are sold in the late fall and early winter. And usually in most stores you can't buy fresh raspberries in January.

Food Cost

How much do you have to spend for food? The cost of food limits what you'll eat. Some foods are too expensive if you don't have much to spend. You may like steak, but you may eat hamburgers more often.

Advertising

How many commercials do you see in a year? Experts say over 10,000! And many are about food. Advertising affects what you eat. A lot of television time is spent convincing you to buy and eat various foods. Food ads are in magazines and on radio, too.

Ads promise that certain foods will make you happy or healthy, but you need to be the judge. Don't believe ads just because you see or hear them. The more you know about food, the better judge you can be.

Knowledge of Food

What you know about food affects what you buy, what you cook, and what you eat. When you know more, you also make wiser food decisions.

This book will teach you many things about food. You'll learn how to choose foods for good health, how to plan meals and snacks, how to shop wisely, and how to prepare food in pleasing ways.

Ads make certain promises. The more you know about food and nutrition the better you can judge the value of this information.

For a healthy and refreshing snack try freezing fruit juice, pudding or yogurt in a paper cup with a wooden stick or plastic spoon. Just pull off the cup and enjoy!

When Do You Eat?

People eat according to their lifestyles. Your *lifestyle* is the way you live. Lifestyles determine when you eat meals and snacks.

Meals

Most people eat three meals a day. They eat breakfast, lunch, and dinner. Others eat four or five mini-meals instead. It doesn't really matter. You do need a variety of foods each day to stay healthy. It's also a good idea to space your meals out.

In many families, adults work and children and teens have after-school and evening activities. They may have jobs, too. And so it's hard to eat as a family. People may eat three meals a day, but they probably don't eat all these meals together.

Snacks

Snacking is common. *Snacks* are foods eaten between meals. At work, people snack on breaks. Students snack after school, especially when they eat an early lunch. Many people snack in the evening while reading a book or while watching TV or a movie.

Snacks are fine if they don't interfere with meals. In fact, they can help keep you healthy. By snacking, you can eat the foods you may have missed at mealtime. As a growing teenager, you may need snack foods to balance your meals.

When do you snack? And what do you eat when you snack? You need to choose snacks wisely.

Most meals are eaten at home and many of them are eaten alone because of busy schedules.

Where Do You Eat?

Food is everywhere! You have many foods to choose from and many places to eat. Where you eat often affects what you eat.

Eating at Home

Most meals are eaten at home. Eating at home is convenient if food is on hand. At home, you can prepare something special. Many people today have casual lifestyles. They may not eat every meal at the table. Instead they may eat by the television, on the patio, or at a kitchen counter.

Eating Out

In the past, almost all meals were eaten at home. That's not true today. Eating out is more common than ever before. People eat one-third of their meals away from home. How many meals have you eaten away from home this week? Meals you eat at school count as meals eaten out.

Besides school, people eat out in restaurants. Today, there are more and more fast-food restaurants. So eating meals and snacks away from home has become quick and handy. Sometimes you have more time and more money. Then you might sit down for a relaxing restaurant meal instead of making a quick trip to a fast-food restaurant.

Think of all the places you eat when you're with friends. Maybe you like to eat a hot dog at a ball game, popcorn at the movies, or frozen yogurt at the shopping mall. Or maybe you buy drinks from vending machines. Foods of all kinds are sold in many places where you go.

Your Food Choices

Throughout your life, you'll make food choices. Your decisions will make a difference in your health and how much you enjoy buying food, cooking, and eating. Take time to learn about food. Then make wise food choices!

Making food choices is a regular part of our lives.

CHAPTER REVIEW

Summary

People eat for many reasons. The most important is to stay alive and keep well. People also eat because food tastes good, food satisfies emotions, and food is part of time spent with others.

Food habits are influenced by your family, your ethnic background, religion, special celebrations, your friends, the region you live in, food costs, the season of the year, advertising, and your knowledge of food.

What Have You Learned?

1. What is wellness?
2. Why do people eat?
3. How might a person's family influence food choices?
4. What is an ethnic food? What is a regional food?
5. Name three holidays and foods that might be eaten to celebrate each.
6. How might friends influence a person's food choices?
7. How does the season of the year influence what people eat?
8. How does advertising affect food choices?
9. Name three different places where you've eaten recently.
10. Is snacking good for you? Explain your answer.

Things to Do

1. List five foods that give you pleasant memories. Write down how these foods make you feel.
2. Tell your classmates about food habits from your family.
3. Go to the grocery store. Write down the names of ten ethnic or regional foods on the shelves. Find out where these foods came from.
4. Find a magazine advertisement about food. Explain what the ad tells you about food. Find out if it's true.
5. Use magazine art to make an illustration of your food habits.

FOOD FOR FITNESS

calorie	a unit for measuring energy
carbohydrates	nutrient which gives energy
combination foods	foods that belong in two or more food groups
digestion	body process of breaking food down into nutrients
empty-calorie foods	foods which provide calories but few nutrients
fat	nutrient which gives energy
food groups	categories of food, grouped because of similar nutrient content
minerals	nutrients that become part of the bones, teeth, and blood and are used by the body in its many processes
nutrients	substances in food which your body uses to keep you well, give you energy, and help you grow
nutrition	the study of nutrients in the food you eat and the way your body uses them
protein	nutrient that helps the body grow and repair
vitamins	nutrients that help direct the way other nutrients and your body work

26

CHAPTER 2

After reading this chapter, you should be able to:

- *state the functions of the leader nutrients.*
- *classify a variety of foods into the food groups.*
- *explain the importance of exercise to health.*

W

hat is good health? When you're healthy, you're fit! Your health affects the way you look, feel, and act. People sometimes say, "You're a picture of health!" This is what they mean:

- You're growing normally.
- You're not too fat or too thin.
- You're energetic and you don't get tired quickly.
- Your teeth are free of cavities.
- Your eyes sparkle.
- Your hair is clean and shiny.
- You're alert.
- You're not sick.

Wellness refers to the total health of your body, your mind and your emotions.

Every part of your body contains protein—even parts you can't see such as your muscles or your lungs.

Wellness is another term for total health of your body, mind, and emotions. It's a popular word many people use today. Keeping well is your responsibility. Often you can stay well more easily than you can cure an illness. Decisions you make every day help prevent health problems now and even years from now.

Your food choices, for example, help keep you healthy. Eating a variety of foods keeps your body running smoothly. *Digestion* is the body process of taking foods that you eat and breaking them down into substances that perform particular jobs to keep you healthy. Getting plenty of exercise and rest helps keep you well, too.

Nutrients in Food

The foods you eat contain substances called *nutrients*. Each nutrient does a special job in keeping you well, giving you energy, and helping you grow. When we talk about *nutrition*, we are talking about the food you eat and the way your body uses the nutrients in the food. When we say a certain food is "nutritious," we mean that it provides you with many important nutrients. Each food contains many different nutrients. There are over 50 different nutrients and your body needs them all! But 50 is a lot to learn about. Even scientists don't know everything about them. Instead you'll learn about several nutrients. These are called leader nutrients. If you get enough of these nutrients each day, you'll probably get the rest of the nutrients you need.

All nutrients are divided into six groups. And they have three major jobs to do:

- Protein—helps your body grow and repair itself.
- Carbohydrate and fat—provide energy.
- Vitamins, minerals, and water—help regulate your body's work.

Protein Helps Your Body Grow and Repair

Protein is a nutrient that helps your body grow and repair itself. It has other jobs too. Look in a mirror. Every part of your body that you see— your skin, your hair, your eyes—is made of protein. Protein is part of everything you can't see, too—your muscles, blood, and organs. Examples of body organs are your lungs, heart, and stomach.

Protein helps your body grow. Students your age are growing very fast. Even if you don't get any taller, your body is still developing. Protein helps people grow to their mature size.

Protein helps with the body's repair work. Your body is made of cells. Every day billions of worn-out cells are replaced, and protein is needed to help make these new cells.

Protein also gives you energy. But that's not its main job. Helping to build and repair your body cells is its major function.

Most foods from animals and a few plant foods are good sources of protein. Nuts, peanut butter, dry beans, and seeds are all foods from plants and good sources of protein.

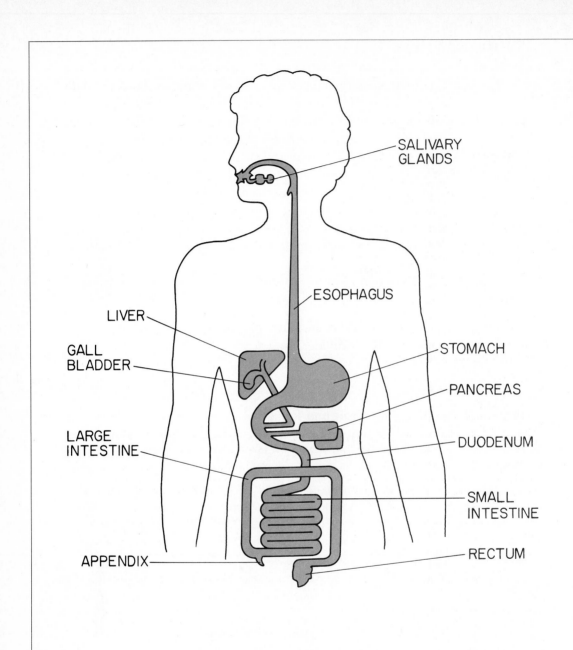

. . . THE DIGESTION ROAD

Have you ever noticed what happens when you bite into food? Saliva suddenly starts to pour into your mouth.

Saliva plays three important roles in digestion. First, it keeps everything in your mouth moist. That makes it easier to chew and to swallow. (Have you ever tried to swallow a mouthful of dry food? Gulp!)

Saliva also helps to begin breaking down food into its nutrients. It does this with chemicals call enzymes. And that's what digestion is all about—breaking food into nutrients for the body to use. And finally, saliva helps food slide down the tube from your mouth to your stomach.

That tube is called the esophagus. The trip down the esophagus doesn't take very long—only a few seconds.

But liquid foods—like milk—make the trip even faster. They can reach your stomach in only 1 second.

Your stomach is like a big balloon. It can stretch itself to hold all the food you pour into it—or almost all. Actually, your stomach can hold about 2 quarts of chewed up food at any one time. Can you imagine how many squished-up sandwiches that would be?

Once the food gets into the stomach, the real work begins. First, digestive juices start pouring out of the stomach's walls, just the way saliva did in your mouth.

Digestive juices break the food into millions of pieces. Digestion can take as long as 3 or 4 hours to turn the food into a soupy mush. Then, the mush moves along to the next step—the small intestine.

Your small intestine really isn't so small. If it were stretched out, it would be about 20 feet long. But in your body, it looks like a coiled-up garden hose. A muscle in the intestine forces the food through—sort of the way you would squeeze a long tube of tooth paste.

Here in your small intestine, more digestive juices break down the mushy food even further. Part of the food is now called nutrients. These nutrients pass through the wall of your small intestine into the bloodstream.

Finally, what's left of the food passes into the large intestine. (Actually, the large intestine isn't all that large. Oh, it's wider than the small intestine, but it's only 5 feet long.)

In the large intestine, digestive juices again work on the mushy food. If there are any nutrients left in the liquid, they and most of the water pass into the bloodstream, too. Everything else passes through the large intestine and out of the body. And that's the end of the line.

Carbohydrate Gives Energy

Carbohydrate is an excellent source of energy. When you move, you use energy. You also need energy to stay alive and to keep your body warm.

The amount of energy food provides your body is measured in *calories*. Consider the way other things are measured. Temperature is measured in degrees. Your height is measured in inches, and your weight, in pounds. The energy in food is measured in calories. In chapter 4, you'll learn more about calories and how your body uses them to make energy.

Two kinds of carbohydrate provide energy—starch and sugar. Carbohydrates come from grain foods, fruits and vegetables, and foods made from sugar. Fiber is another kind of carbohydrate that you need to stay healthy. Fiber helps food move through your body during digestion. It comes from fruits, vegetables, nuts, dry beans, and whole-grain breads and cereals.

Fat Gives Energy

Fat is another nutrient that gives energy. It provides calories, too. Fat gives more calories than an equal amount of carbohydrate would.

As a nutrient, fat has other functions:

- It adds flavor to food.
- It helps satisfy your hunger because fat stays in your stomach longer than other nutrients do.
- It promotes growth and healthy skin.

Where does fat come from? Some foods such as butter, salad dressing, vegetable oil, and margarine are mostly fat. Other foods such as nuts, peanut butter, meat, and cheese have some fat in them along with many other nutrients.

Although fat is important, too much isn't good for you. It can lead to weight problems and heart disease when you're older. Most people get more than enough fat in their meals and snacks.

Vitamins Help Regulate

Vitamins are nutrients that help your body do its work. Even though your body only needs tiny amounts of each vitamin, they are essential to life. The name "vitamin" comes from the Greek word for life, "vita"!

Vitamins are regulators. A stoplight is a regulator, too. It directs the flow of traffic. Vitamins help direct the way other nutrients and the body work. There are many different vitamins. Each regulates body processes in a different way. Vitamins are named after the letters of the alphabet. Some important vitamins are vitamin A, the B vitamins, and vitamin C.

Vitamin A   Did you ever walk into a dark room after you'd been in the bright sunlight? Vitamin A helps your eyes adjust to the dark. It comes from dark-green, leafy vegetables and yellow fruits and vegetables.

B Vitamins   The B vitamins are grouped together because their jobs are similar. They all help your body use energy from carbohydrate, fat, and protein. These nutrients keep your body healthy in other ways, too. For example, they help keep your eyes, skin, and hair healthy.

B vitamins come from different foods. Thiamine, also called vitamin B_1, and niacin, another B vitamin, come mainly from meat, dry beans, breads, and cereals. Riboflavin, or vitamin B_2, comes from milk and many foods made from milk.

Vitamin C   When you cut or bruise yourself, vitamin C helps the wound heal. It also helps you stay well. Vitamin C helps keep your gums healthy too. Then you'll have a nicer smile throughout your life.

Vitamin C comes from fruits, such as oranges, berries, and melon. Some dark-green vegetables such as spinach have vitamin C, too.

These foods are all good sources of Vitamin C.

HOW NUTRIENTS WORK FOR YOU

Each nutrient has a certain job to do. But all nutrients work together as a team. If one nutrient is missing, it can keep another from working properly!

What They Do	Good Food Sources
Protein ■ Builds and repairs the body ■ Supplies energy	Meat, eggs, fish, poultry, milk, cheese, yogurt, dry beans, peanuts, nuts, seeds
Carbohydrate ■ Supplies energy ■ Provides fiber	Breads, cereals, rice, pasta, fruit, vegetables, sugar, other sweets
Fat ■ Provides energy ■ Adds flavor to food ■ Helps satisfy the appetite ■ Helps promote growth and healthy skin	Oil, butter, margarine, salad dressing, meat, cheese, nuts, peanut butter
Vitamins *Vitamin A* ■ *Helps eyes adjust to darkness* ■ *Helps keep skin healthy*	Dark green vegetables, yellow vegetables and fruits, eggs
B Vitamins (thiamine, riboflavin, niacin) ■ Helps carbohydrates, fat, and protein produce energy ■ Helps keep eyes, skin, and hair healthy	Meat, poultry, fish, eggs, whole-grain and enriched breads and cereals, milk, cheese, yogurt, ice cream
Vitamin C ■ Helps keep gums healthy ■ Helps wounds heal ■ Helps the body fight infection	Oranges, grapefruit, other citrus fruit, berries, melon, broccoli, potatoes, tomatoes, cabbage
Minerals *Calcium* ■ Helps build strong, healthy teeth and bones ■ Helps the heart beat properly ■ Helps muscles move	Milk, cheese, yogurt, ice cream, green-leafy vegetables, fish with tiny bones
Iron ■ Helps the blood carry oxygen ■ Helps cells use oxygen	Meat, eggs, liver, dry beans, whole-grain and enriched breads, and cereals
Water ■ Carries nutrients through the body ■ Helps regulate body processes ■ Helps maintain normal body temperature	Beverages, soup, drinking water, many fruits and vegetables

Minerals Help Regulate

Like vitamins, minerals often act as regulators, used by the body in its many processes. They, too, are essential even though they are needed in much smaller amounts than protein, carbohydrate, and fat. Unlike vitamins, minerals actually become part of your body in its bones, teeth, and blood. There are about 20 known minerals. By eating a variety of foods daily, you should get the minerals you need. Two minerals you should know about are calcium and iron.

Calcium   Calcium really has two basic jobs. Ninety-nine percent of your body's calcium is in your bones and teeth. Getting enough calcium while you're growing helps bones become longer and stronger. The way you feed your bones now pays off when you're an adult. You'll be less likely to get bone disease which causes them to break easily. Calcium is also a regulator. It helps muscles move and helps the heart beat.

The best source of calcium is dairy foods. Some green leafy vegetables and fish eaten with their bones, such as sardines or canned salmon, have calcium too.

Iron   The nutrient iron becomes part of your blood. Iron helps carry the oxygen you breathe to your muscles, your brain, and in fact, to every part of your body. Oxygen is necessary to help your body make the energy it needs to keep you going. Teenagers, especially, need plenty of iron.

The best source of iron is liver. But iron also comes from meat, eggs, dry beans, and some breads and cereals.

Most of Your Body Is Water

Water is a nutrient, too! You can't live without it. In fact, water makes up about two-thirds of your body. For example, blood is mainly water. And every other body cell contains water, too. Water is another regulator. It carries nutrients to every part of your body. It also helps keep your body at just the right temperature. You need water every day to replace what you lose. You lose water in sweat, your breath, and in urine.

Almost everything you eat and drink contains water. Milk, juice, and soup are mostly water. That doesn't surprise you. But did you know that lettuce, apples, bananas, and cooked beef are more than half water, too?

Water is a nutrient too. Its primary job is to carry other nutrients to all parts of your body.

Food Groups

People need nutrients, and food provides them. Different foods contain different nutrients. For example, milk is a good source of calcium and protein, but it doesn't have much vitamin C like many fruits do. That's why you need a variety of foods every day.

Foods are divided into five food groups according to the nutrients they contain. The four main food groups are the Milk and Cheese Group, the Meat, Poultry, Fish, and Beans Group, the Fruit and Vegetable Group, and the Bread and Cereal Group. Eating a variety of foods from each of these four groups provides a variety of the nutrients you need for good health. The fifth group is the Fats and Sweets Group which provides few nutrients and many calories. You do not need foods from this group to maintain good health.

Milk and Cheese Group

Foods that belong to the Milk and Cheese Group are good sources of protein, calcium, and riboflavin. Do you remember what these nutrients do? Foods in the Milk and Cheese Group are all made from milk. What foods might belong in this group? You're right if you said yogurt, cheese, cottage cheese, ice cream, pudding, and milkshakes.

Foods from these four food groups every day will provide you with all the nutrients you need.

Meat, Poultry, Fish, and Beans Group

The Meat, Poultry, Fish, and Beans Group is a good source of four nutrients—protein, thiamine, niacin, and iron. Check again to see what these nutrients do.

What foods belong in this group? Beef, pork, lamb, liver, chicken, fish, and eggs do. Chicken and turkey are two kinds of poultry. Dry beans, nuts, peanut butter, and seeds do, too. Do you know why? All of these foods are good sources of the same nutrients. So, on a sandwich, you can substitute peanut butter for beef and still eat a nutritious meal.

People who don't eat meat, chicken, or fish are called vegetarians. They can get the nutrients they need from this food group from other foods in the same group. They can substitute eggs, peanut butter, seeds, and nuts.

Fruit and Vegetable Group

Most vegetables and fruits in the Fruit and Vegetable Group are good sources of either vitamin A, vitamin C, or both. Fruits and vegetables give you fiber, too. What do these nutrients and fiber do?

These foods in the Fruit and Vegetable Group are good sources of vitamin C: oranges, grapefruit, berries, melons, tomatoes, cabbage, and green peppers. These are some good sources of vitamin A: greens, carrots, broccoli, sweet potatoes, tomatoes, green peppers, and apricots.

Bread and Cereal Group

The Bread and Cereal Group is a good source of carbohydrate, thiamine, niacin, and iron. How do these nutrients help your body do its work? Whole-grain breads and cereals are good sources of fiber, too.

Many foods made from grains belong in this group. This includes tortillas, bagels, waffles, biscuits, breakfast cereal, grits, pasta, rice, and many kinds of bread. How many kinds of bread can you name?

Fats and Sweets Group

Many foods in the Fats and Sweets Group have carbohydrate and fat. What job do these nutrients do? You're right if you said that they provide energy, or calories.

Foods in the Fats and Sweets Group have few, if any, other nutrients. For this reason, foods with only carbohydrate and fat are often called *empty-calorie* foods. You can get carbohydrate and fat *plus* many other valuable nutrients from the foods in the four main food groups. When we talk of good nutrition we talk of the four food groups. Can you name these four food groups?

What kind of foods belong in the Fats and Sweets Group? Foods that don't belong anywhere else do:

- foods high in fat, such as butter, margarine, oil, and salad dressing
- foods high in sugar, such as candy, soft drinks, syrup, honey, jelly, cakes, and cookies
- foods such as catsup and mustard that don't have many nutrients at all

Combination Foods

What food group does pizza belong in? A hamburger? Beef stew? These foods don't belong in just one food group. They belong in two or more groups, so they are called *combination foods*. Nutrients in a combination food represent several food groups, too. Pizza, for example, has foods from all four food groups:

- The crust belongs in the Bread and Cereal Group.
- The sausage belongs in the Meat, Poultry, Fish, and Beans Group.
- The mushrooms and green peppers are part of the Fruit and Vegetable Group.
- The cheese belongs in the Milk and Cheese Group.

Pizza is a good source of all the nutrients you've learned about. Try to name the nutrients provided by each food in a pizza.

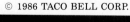

© 1986 TACO BELL CORP.

Combination foods contain foods from two or more of the main four food groups.

Vitamin Pills—Who Needs Them?

If you're eating nutritious foods, do you need vitamin pills, too? You probably don't.

Vitamins do promote health. And eating a variety of foods from the four main food groups can provide all the vitamins you need. Extra vitamins just won't make you extra healthy! In fact, taking too many can be dangerous.

Who uses vitamin pills then? Doctors sometimes prescribe vitamin pills. But they're recommended for special health reasons, perhaps during pregnancy or long illnesses. Remember that vitamin pills can never replace food. Only food has all the nutrients you need to stay well. Take vitamin pills only if a doctor tells you to.

If you eat foods from the four food groups everyday you won't need vitamin pills. Extra vitamins don't make you extra healthy or give you added energy.

Exercise is just as important to good health as is a balanced diet.

Exercise—As Important as Nutrition

Like nutrition, exercise helps keep you fit. For good health, you need to strike a balance. Plan both vigorous exercise along with some quiet time for yourself.

What is exercise? Exercise takes many forms. Jumping jacks, sit ups, and push-ups certainly are exercises. So are playing soccer, swimming, and skating. Even a fast walk to a friend's house a mile away is good exercise. Every time your muscles work hard you're exercising them.

Exercise for Health

Why is exercise so important?

- It helps build strong muscles which give your body shape.
- It makes your body more flexible. Then you can move more gracefully.
- It helps make your lungs and heart strong. Did you know that your heart is a muscle, too? And it needs exercise.
- It helps you control your weight.
- It helps you relax. And that makes you feel good all over!

For good health, exercise three or four times a week. It's a good habit to get into. Exercise is an important habit that should follow you throughout life.

Food and Exercise

Food and exercise are tied together. If you exercise regularly, you may need more food than someone who sits most of the time. Because you use more energy, you need more energy from food. Generally, your appetite is bigger, too. So you naturally eat more.

Besides needing more calories, exercise really doesn't change the nutrients you need. You still need a variety of foods from the four main food groups.

Have you noticed how much you sweat when you exercise a lot? Maybe you ran really fast, bicycled up a steep hill, or even danced a long time. When you sweat, your body loses water. You need to replace that water right away so you don't get dehydrated. Dehydration is a very serious body condition. Being thirsty is a body signal that says, "I need water."

Some people think they need extra salt when they exercise a lot, so they take salt tablets. Salt contains a mineral called sodium. You lose some sodium when you sweat. Foods have plenty of sodium already. You don't need any extra.

If you're involved in a special athletic program, eat a variety of foods from the four main food groups. That's best for training. You need the nutrients from many different foods for both energy and growth.

TRUE OR FALSE?

Eating chocolate causes pimples.
False. Neither do drinking soft drinks or eating french fries. Although a variety of food promotes healthy skin, food doesn't cause pimples. The changes in your body during your teenage years and your emotions can cause skin problems.

Vitamin pills will give me energy.
False. Energy comes from three nutrients—carbohydrate, fat, and protein. Vitamins don't provide these, so they can't give you a boost of energy.

Eating gelatin can make my fingernails grow stronger.
False. This is an old myth. Gelatin, a kind of protein, won't have much effect on your fingernails.

The more protein I eat, the stronger I'll get.
False. You're right to know that protein is part of your muscles. But eating extra protein doesn't give you extra strength. Only exercise can do that.

Once I stop growing, I can stop drinking milk.
False. The nutrients in milk help your bones grow. Interestingly, bones can keep growing stronger until you're in your 30's. Even after that, you need milk's nutrients to keep your bones strong.

Testing for Nutrients in Class

Scientists learn about water and other nutrients in food by conducting experiments. In this way, they learn which foods are good sources of each nutrient. In class, you can conduct experiments to find nutrients in various foods as well.

Testing for Fat

Fat is a nutrient in some, but not all, foods. These are the steps to follow when you test for fat in food:

- Gather the supplies for this demonstration. You'll need brown paper, pen or pencil, and margarine. You'll also need small amounts of other foods to test, such as: apple slice, potato, green bean, cheese cube, drop of skim milk, cracker, bread, bacon, peanut, potato chip, donut, drop of vegetable oil, and drop of soft drink.
- First, rub some margarine on brown paper. You know that margarine is mainly fat.
- Now hold the paper up to the light. What do you see? Margarine leaves a translucent spot. That means that the spot is clear enough to allow the sun's rays to pass through. The reason that margarine leaves a spot is that is contains the nutrient fat.
- Rub pieces of several other foods on the paper. Under each rubbing, write the name of the food. Your group may test all the foods mentioned in the first step, or just the few assigned by your teacher.
- Let the paper dry for a few minutes. The fat won't dry, but the water will.
- Now hold the paper up to the light again. Circle the names of the foods that seem to contain fat.

The spot you see on the brown paper is caused by the fat in the food that was rubbed on the paper.

Studying the Test Results

A scientist always studies the information from an experiment, then tries to answer questions. Study the information from the fat demonstration, then answer these questions.

- What foods have fat as a key nutrient in food?
- What can you say about the nutrients in food? Do they all have the same nutrients?
- Which food groups might provide fat?
- You tested several foods from the same food group. What results show you that nutrients in a food group might differ slightly?
- You tested a potato and a potato chip. Why does one form of potato contain fat, but not both? Find out where the fat came from.

Besides fat, you can test foods in your food lab to find other nutrients. Your teacher can give you the directions. As you conduct your tests, you'll see that different foods have different nutrients. That's why variety among your food choices is so very important. Food, along with exercise, helps keep you healthy!

CHAPTER REVIEW

Summary

Nutrition and exercise promote wellness. Healthy people look and feel good. Nutrients in food help keep people healthy. Each nutrient has specific jobs in the body.

Foods are classified into five food groups because of their nutrient content. The main four food groups are the Milk and Cheese Group; the Meat, Poultry, Fish, and Beans Group; the Fruit and Vegetable Group; and the Bread and Cereal Group. Foods in the fifth group—the Fats and Sweets Group—are not necessary because they are high in calories and low in nutrients other than fat. People need to eat a variety of foods from the four food groups to stay healthy.

What Have You Learned?

1. What do you need to stay healthy?
2. What nutrients give you energy?
3. What job does protein do in your body? Carbohydrate? Fat? Vitamins? Minerals? Water?
4. What are calories?
5. Name the four main food groups. For each group name three types of food that belong in that group.
6. Name the major nutrients in each of the main four food groups.
7. What are combination foods?
8. What are empty-calorie foods? What food group do they belong in?
9. How does exercise benefit your health?

Things to Do

1. Make your own food group poster. Use magazine pictures of foods from the four main food groups. Include the nutrient names contributed by each food group.
2. Create a crossword puzzle using words about nutrition from this chapter. Write the answers on a separate paper, then swap puzzles with another student.

PLANNING MEALS AND SNACKS

balanced diet	daily menus which meet the recommendations of the Daily Food Guide
budget	a plan for spending the money you have
Daily Food Guide	guideline for planning and judging a day's menu plan
garnish	food used to decorate another food
menu	a list of foods to be served at a meal
schedule	a plan for how you will spend your time

CHAPTER 3

After reading this chapter, you should be able to:

- *name at least five things to consider when planning a menu.*
- *plan a meal which appeals to the senses.*
- *plan a day's menu which meets the guidelines of the Daily Food Guide.*
- *list nutritious and empty-calorie snacks.*

"W hat's on the menu today?" You've probably heard that question in restaurants, and maybe at home. It's a question you may have asked yourself.

A *menu* is a list of foods served at one meal. Several menus make up the plan for all the meals and snacks served in a day, or even a week.

Planning Makes Perfect!

Good menus don't just happen. They're planned. Many factors go into planning meals and snacks.

Well-planned menus taste and look good, and they include the variety of foods and nutrients which keep you healthy. They're enjoyable, too! Let's learn how to plan successful meals and snacks.

Meals for Different People

Meals and snacks are planned to consider the different needs of people. A good menu plan shows that you've considered all the details: how many people, their ages, their food likes and dislikes, and when they can eat.

How Many?   How many people will eat the meals and snacks you plan? This information is important to know before you:

- choose recipes.
- buy food.
- prepare food.
- set the table.

Recipes are directions for making certain foods. Some are right for serving one or two people. Others are better for a large group, perhaps ten or twelve.

Knowing how many people will eat helps you know how much food to buy and prepare. You want to have enough to eat. But you won't want too much leftover food unless you have plans for it.

Before arranging the table, know how many places to set. People feel welcome when they all have a place to sit. And you won't have to scurry setting extra dishes and utensils at the last minute.

We usually think of families when we think of meal planning. But someone has to plan school lunch menus just as someone has to plan the menus for patients in a hospital. You'll learn more about those careers in Chapter 16.

Their Ages   In chapter 2, you learned that people need the same nutrients. But they need different amounts of these nutrients depending on their age, so they eat different amounts of food.

The amount of food you prepare depends on how much people eat. Small children eat less than teenagers and adults. People your age are growing very fast! You probably eat more than a younger brother or sister does. Most teenagers eat more than their parents and grandparents, too.

People of varying ages may need different kinds of foods, too. Babies don't have many teeth so they can't chew very well. Their young bodies can't digest all the foods you eat either. Preschoolers usually like plain foods. Six-year-olds with their front teeth missing can't bite into apples. Sometimes older adults need special foods too, especially if they have health problems. How can you make one meal suit everyone? It's easy. Just plan to:

- chop or mash meat and vegetables for babies. They can't eat spicy foods such as pizza. Instead serve them simply prepared foods.
- give second helpings and possibly add extra bread to meals for teens. This will satisfy their hearty appetites.
- serve smaller portions to adults who don't get much exercise. Perhaps you could give them a lower calorie dessert, such as a piece of fruit instead of apple pie. Or you could give them a smaller piece of pie.

Their Likes and Dislikes   What are your favorite foods? What foods don't you like as much? Everybody has food likes and dislikes. A wise menu planner knows what foods people prefer. You please them when you serve their favorites.

Good menus may include new foods which people haven't tasted before. Serve a new food in a meal along with more familiar foods.

Older adults who don't get much exercise need less food and fewer calories than teenagers or adults. Serve them smaller portions or substitute fruit for high calorie desserts.

Before you shop know how much you can spend—or what your budget is. Some foods are more expensive than others. For example steak costs more than hamburger. So you might want to save steak for special occasions.

Their Schedules Successful meals and snacks need to be planned to match family schedules. A *schedule* is a plan for how you will spend your time. Each family has a different schedule.

When a family eats together, menu planning is easy. But sometimes, busy schedules mean that everyone eats at a different time. When that happens, plan foods that reheat easily. Or perhaps serve cold foods that keep in the refrigerator.

Your Food Budget

A good menu is planned to match the food budget. A *budget* is a plan for spending your money. Before you plan, decide how much you can spend on a meal. Then you know how much and what kinds of foods you can buy. The price of food depends on many things:

- Some foods are more expensive because the supply is limited. A beef steak, for example is more expensive than ground beef. Asparagus is more expensive than green beans.
- Prepared foods usually cost more than foods you cook yourself. For example, you pay more for frozen waffles than for waffles you make from scratch.
- The season of the year makes a difference in the price of fresh fruits and vegetables. They're least expensive during the time they are picked or harvested. Strawberries, for example, are cheapest in late spring.

Some foods are only available during certain seasons. At that time they're usually inexpensive. It's a good time to include them in your meal plans.

Available Foods

What's cooking? It all depends on what foods you can get. The foods you include in your plan might already be in your kitchen, or they might be foods you can buy at the store. If they're not available they shouldn't be in your plan.

Foods in Your Kitchen Look in the cabinet, the refrigerator, and the freezer. Know what you have on hand before you plan menus! Use those foods first along with any food left from other meals.

Foods at the Stores Plan the rest of the menu to include foods you can buy. That may sound like common sense. But remember:

- Some foods are sold only at certain times of the year. For example, in most places, you can't buy watermelon in winter.
- Some stores are too small to sell all the foods you might want. For example, they might not sell foods for Chinese cooking.

Your Food Preparation Time

Before you start planning, know how much time you have to prepare meals. When you have lots of time, you may want to plan an elaborate meal. Then you can serve foods that take longer to prepare and cook, like roast beef does. When time is short, plan something quick and easy. A hamburger or cheese sandwich cooks fast.

Planning ahead helps you use your food preparation time wisely. For example, shopping ahead is a timesaver. You don't want to have to take the time to run to the store every time you prepare a meal.

Meals with Appeal

A well-planned meal really can make your mouth water. Close your eyes, and imagine your favorite meal. It looks good, smells good, and tastes delicious! In fact, it probably appeals to all of your five senses.

Variety makes meals appealing. Meals look and taste better when there are many different flavors, colors, shapes and sizes, textures, and temperatures of foods.

Flavors A meal that tastes good has many different flavors. And it has a variety of foods, too.

A good planning rule is to avoid repeating the same food. Cheese soup and a toasted cheese sandwich at one meal are too much alike. You might serve tomato soup instead.

Color A good-looking meal is like a picture. Different colors add interest. A meal that's all one color looks boring.

Which meal is more interesting to look at? Dinner #1 is a pork chop, cauliflower, rice, a biscuit, and milk. Dinner #2 is barbecued chicken, broccoli, carrot-raisin salad, cornbread, and milk. You're right if you said dinner #2. It's more colorful.

Why is menu #2 more appealing? How could you make menu #1 more attractive?

Shape and Size   An attractive meal has foods prepared in different sizes and shapes. Long string beans and long french fries wouldn't look good together on a plate. But the same beans would look nice with potato rounds or small, whole potatoes.

By cutting, you can change the size and shape of food. For example, you can cut carrots into rounds or sticks. Or you can grate them into tiny pieces. A bread slice can be cut into squares or triangles.

Texture   A food's texture is the way it feels. It may be smooth, crunchy, stringy, soft or hard, tender or tough. A variety of textures makes a meal more interesting.

Pretend that dinner is split pea soup, beef hash, mashed potatoes, cottage cheese, and fruit juice. Would this meal have much interest? The answer is "no." All the foods have the same smooth texture. In addition, there's not much variety of color.

You can add a crunchy texture to smooth foods to add interest. Sprinkle nuts on vegetables, sunflower seeds on salads, or granola on yogurt.

Temperature   A well-planned meal usually has both hot and cold foods for interest. Ice cream is a nice cold dessert for a hot meal. And hot soup is a nice contrast to a cold sandwich.

At serving time, remember that hot foods taste best hot, and cold foods are more refreshing when they're cold. These same foods served at room temperature aren't as good.

Using both hot and cold foods in a meal makes it more interesting.

Garnishes Garnishes make foods more interesting, too. A *garnish* is a food which adds decoration to another food. Garnishes can be very simple. For example, a baked potato is more interesting sprinkled with grated cheese and paprika. The cheese and paprika are garnishes. A sprig of green parsley adds color to macaroni and cheese. And a lemon slice on the rim of a glass of lemonade adds a different shape as well as color.

Meals for Good Health

Most important, a well-planned menu provides nutrients for growth, energy, and health. Do you remember what nutrients are? They're the substances which make up food. Each nutrient has a specific and important job in your body. By eating a variety of foods, you get the nutrients you need.

Food Groups: A Menu Planning Guide

One way to decide if your diet is nutritious is to add up the nutrients in every food. But that takes time. Here's an easier way! Follow the Daily Food Guide. The *Daily Food Guide* is a simple guide for planning and judging food choices.

Daily meals and snacks which follow the Daily Food Guide are balanced. This means that they provide both the variety and amount of nutrients people need each day. By definition, a *balanced diet plan* meets the recommendations of the Daily Food Guide.

What's in a balanced diet? It has the recommended number of servings from each of the four main food groups. Chapter 2 listed the foods in each group. Now you'll learn how much you need from each food group!

MEALS FROM THE DAILY FOOD GUIDE

Milk and Cheese Group	Meat, Fish, Poultry, and Beans Group	Vegetable and Fruit Group	Bread and Cereal Group	Fats and Sweets Group
yogurt	sausage	strawberries	pancakes	syrup
cottage cheese	tuna	apple juice banana	whole-wheat bread	cookie
milk	barbecued chicken	corn-on-the-cob coleslaw	biscuits	butter
cheese	refried beans	lettuce and tomato	tortilla	soft drink

Foods in the Milk and Cheese Group.
- Adults need 2 servings a day.

- Children need 3 servings a day.

- Teenagers need 4 servings a day.

Milk and Cheese Group

Do you remember what foods belong in the Milk and Cheese Group? You're right if you said foods made from milk.

Butter, cream, and sour cream are three exceptions. Do you know why they don't belong? These foods don't have the nutrients that milk has. They don't have much protein, calcium, phosphorus, or riboflavin. They are mainly fat. And so they belong in the Fats and Sweets Group.

The number of servings you need each day from the Milk and Cheese Group depends on your age. If you're twelve or under, you need at least three servings. Teenagers need at least four. And most adults need at least two. Adults don't need as much because they've stopped growing, but you never outgrow your need for the nutrients foods in the Milk and Cheese Group provide.

Serving size is important to know. How much is one serving from the Milk and Cheese Group? Each of these serving sizes gives the same amount of calcium:

- 1 cup milk
- 1 cup yogurt
- 1 cup pudding
- 2 cups cottage cheese
- 1 ½ slices cheese
- 1 ¾ cup ice cream

Meat, Poultry, Fish, and Beans Group

Can you name the foods in the Meat, Poultry, Fish, and Beans Group? Remember that eggs belong in this group and so do dry beans, peanuts, nuts, and seeds.

Children, teens, and adults need two servings daily from the Meat, Poultry, Fish, and Beans Group. How much is one serving? It's not as big as you might think. One serving of cooked meat is two ounces. That's a little smaller than the palm of your hand!

Any one of the following equals a serving that will give you the same amount of protein as two ounces of cooked meat, fish, or chicken:

- 2 eggs
- ¼ cup peanut butter
- 1 cup cooked, dry beans
- ½ cup nuts

Fruit and Vegetable Group

People need four servings from the Fruit and Vegetable Group daily. Besides that rule of thumb, plan to eat at least one vitamin C-rich food each day and one vitamin A-rich food every other day. Know what foods are high in vitamin A and which ones are good sources of vitamin C. Breakfast is a good time to eat a food high in vitamin C. What could you have? Orange juice, strawberries, and cantaloupe are three good choices. A serving from the Fruit and Vegetable Group could be any of the following:

- ½ cup fruit juice
- 1 medium-size fruit
- ½ cup cooked vegetables
- 1 cup raw vegetables or fruit

Bread and Cereal Group

Foods in the Bread and Cereal Group are made from grain. How many different foods from this group can you name? Everyone needs four servings each day from the Bread and Cereal Group. Any one of the following examples is equal to one serving from this food group:

- 1 slice bread
- 1 cup dry breakfast cereal
- ½ cup cooked cereal or grits
- ½ cup rice or pasta

We need 2 servings a day from the Meat, Fish, Poultry and Beans Group.

We all need 4 servings a day from the Fruit and Vegetable Group.

We need 4 servings a day from the Bread and Cereal Group.

Fats and sweets add flavor to our foods but we must be careful that we don't eat too many of these empty calories.

Fats and Sweets Group

How many servings do you need each day from the Fats and Sweets Group? You don't need any. Instead, be careful that you don't eat too much from this group. Small amounts of foods in this group can add flavor and variety to meal and snack choices. If you don't eat too many, you can enjoy these empty-calorie foods.

Combination Foods

You remember that combination foods belong in two or more food groups. A taco, a hamburger, and pizza are all combination foods. The foods they're made from belong in several food groups. Combination foods may provide a whole serving. Or they may give just part of a serving from each food group.

How many servings from the four main food groups does this peanut butter sandwich have? It has two tablespoons of peanut butter on a slice of toast. The answer is one-half serving from the Meat, Poultry, Fish, and Beans Group and one serving from the Bread and Cereal Group.

Balanced Menus for a Day

All meals and snacks eaten in a day provide you with your daily intake of nutrients. Each day try to eat the kinds and amounts of food that provide you with all the nutrients your body needs. Follow the guidelines of the Daily Food Guide.

Breakfast, Lunch, Dinner

Good meals usually have a variety of foods. They also have foods from each of the four main food groups.

The chart, "How Do These Meals Compute?" shows three meals and a snack with foods from the first four food groups. Some have a food from the Fats and Sweets Group, too. Think of another meal that could be added to this chart.

HOW DO THESE MEALS COMPUTE?

This is a day's menu for you. Does it have enough food from the Daily Food Guide?

Breakfast
1 cup corn flakes
1 sliced banana
1 cup milk

Lunch
toasted cheese sandwich (1 slice cheese on two slices bread)
4 celery sticks
1 apple
1 cup chocolate milk

Dinner
3 ounce cooked chicken breast
½ cup broccoli
½ cup brown rice
1 cup milk
1 slice chocolate cake

Snack
¼ cup peanuts

Good Snacks

Snacks can add a lot of nutrients. There are many good snack foods from each food group. See if you can put the foods in the chart, "Which Snack for You?," into the four food groups. What other snack foods belong in these groups?

Snack foods also come from the Fats and Sweets Group. These foods add extra calories, or energy, to your menu plan. What are some foods from this group? You're right if you said chips, soft drinks, candy, cookies, and cake.

Since you're growing, you can use the calories that come from these foods, as long as you're not overweight. But the best guideline is to eat a balanced diet first. Then occasionally include a snack from the Fats and Sweets Group.

WHICH SNACK FOR YOU?

Can you put these nutritious snacks into the four main food groups? **Hint**: Some snacks are combination foods.

cheese	chicken leg	cheese pizza
crackers	toast	raisins
banana	milk	green pepper
celery sticks	hard-cooked eggs	tacos
sunflower seeds	apple juice	ice cream
milkshakes	nuts	apple
yogurt	peanut butter sandwich	granola

These family members all have different food needs. Consider those needs as you plan menus for a day.

Menu Planning in Class

Menu planning takes practice. Plan menus for a specific family for one day. Include all meals and snacks. You might do this alone or with a group of students. This is the family you'll plan the day's menus for:

- **mother.** She's 35 years old. She works from 9 a.m. until 1 p.m. in an office. She likes most foods, especially salads.
- **father.** He's 38 years old. He works full time from 8 a.m. until 5:30 p.m. as a carpenter. He likes beef stew and other hearty meals.
- **brother.** He's 14 years old and growing! He's in school from 7:30 a.m. until 3:30 p.m. Tonight he has play practice starting at 6:30 p.m. He loves peanut butter sandwiches.
- **sister.** She's 10 years old. She's in school from 8:30 a.m. until 3:00 p.m. Tonight she has a piano lesson from 6 to 7 p.m. Her favorite food is any kind of fruit.
- **baby.** She's 9 months old. She stays with a sitter from 8:30 a.m. until 1:30 p.m. She still eats soft and finely-chopped foods.

Start by writing down information about the people who will be eating. Determine how many there are, their ages, the things they do, their schedules, and their favorite foods.

Then make a daily menu plan that's right for them. Plan to pack lunches for dad, brother, and sister. Check your plan against the Daily Food Guide. Do you have enough servings from each of the main food groups? Remember that snacks can help them meet the guidelines.

And last, look at your menu carefully. Does it have enough variety? Will the food look appealing? If not, make some changes!

A well-planned menu includes foods people will eat and enjoy. Careful planning is important!

FOOD TIPS FOR BABY-SITTERS

Baby-sitters are often responsible for feeding children. Know that youngsters eat differently than grown-ups. Always have the parents show you what foods to feed their children.

Infants
- Feed a baby in a high chair or on your lap.
- Warm a baby's bottle of milk or formula. But don't make it hot. You can check the temperature by turning the bottle upside down and shaking a couple of drops onto your wrist.
- Serve food warm or at room temperature. It might need to be chopped or mashed.
- Put just a little food on the spoon at a time.
- Burp the baby halfway through a meal and when the meal is over.
- Throw away what the baby doesn't eat from the bowl or bottle.

Children
- Serve small servings.
- Keep the food plain and simple.
- Cut food in small pieces for them if they're young.
- Give them finger foods.
- Give them plenty of time to eat.

CHAPTER REVIEW

Summary

A well-planned menu considers many facts about the people eating. The number of people, their ages, their likes and dislikes, and their schedules are all important. Meals that look and taste good have variety in color, texture, shape, flavor, and temperature. Garnishes make foods look nicer.

A balanced daily menu provides the nutrients people need for energy, growth, and health. A variety of foods from the food groups is important. A day's meals and snacks are balanced when they meet Daily Food Guide recommendations.

What Have You Learned?

1. How do each of these things affect menu planning: number of people, their ages, their schedules, and their food likes and dislikes?
2. How can you make a meal look and taste good?
3. What are three simple food garnishes?
4. Why is variety important in planning menus?
5. Why should you use the Daily Food Guide to plan meals and snacks?
6. How much should teenagers eat daily from each group in the Daily Food Guide? How is this different for children twelve and under?
7. There are no recommendations for the Fats and Sweets Group. Why not?
8. Name four nutritious snacks and four empty-calorie snacks. How do they differ?

Things to Do

1. Find pictures in magazines of five garnishes on food. Tell why they make the food more interesting.
2. Plan menus for a day, including snacks that you would eat. They should meet the guidelines from the Daily Food Guide.
3. Look in cookbooks to find recipes for nutritious snacks. Find one recipe for each main food group and write it down.

WEIGHT CONTROL

anorexia	an eating behavior in which people have such a fear of being fat that they severely starve themselves
bulimia	an eating behavior in which people overeat then vomit to rid their body of food
diet	all foods people eat and drink
fad diet	a diet often for losing weight, that is very popular only for a short time, but people soon find will not be satisfactory
pinch test	way to estimate body fat by pinching together the skin on certain areas of your body

CHAPTER 4

After reading this chapter, you should be able to:

- *explain how the body uses calories.*
- *identify low-calorie and high-calorie foods.*
- *describe ways to control calories in your food choices.*
- *explain how exercise helps control weight.*
- *judge a fad diet.*
- *show awareness of anorexia and bulimia.*

W

hen you feel good about yourself, you enjoy life more and you enjoy others more. You're also more likely to succeed! Being your own best weight is part of feeling good.

People come in all different sizes and shapes.

What's Your Best Weight?

People come in different sizes and shapes. No one size or shape is better than another. Your best weight is what's right for you. For example, people with bigger bones weigh more than people with small bones and taller people weigh more than shorter people. And muscular people weigh more than those with less muscle as long as their builds are similar.

Weight isn't really the issue, how much body fat you have is. Being too fat or too thin isn't healthy. Too much fat puts a needless strain on the body. In the long run, it can cause problems for the heart and other body organs.

Being too fat or too thin can also keep people from doing things they enjoy. They may feel uncomfortable or unattractive. Sometimes other people tease them or treat them unfairly.

You can estimate your body fat with a *pinch test.* Pinch your skin on your side just above your waist or on the back of your upper arm. If you can pinch more than an inch, you probably have too much body fat. If you pinch less than one-half inch, you may not have enough.

Let a doctor be the real judge of your weight. It's very easy to overestimate your body fat. If you're just a little under weight or overweight, you can control calories on your own. If you need to gain or lose quite a few pounds, let a doctor plan a diet that's right for you. A *diet* is all the food you eat and drink.

The pinch test is one way to determine if you're overweight.

The Calorie Story

Calories are a unit of energy. They measure the amount of energy in food. And they measure the energy your body uses.

TRUE OR FALSE?

Potatoes are high-calorie foods.
False. A baked or boiled potato doesn't have many calories by itself. But calories add up when you put butter or sour cream on top.

Toast has fewer calories than bread.
False. Toasting can't change the calories in food. Water is the only nutrient lost. And water doesn't have calories!

Margarine has less calories than butter.
False. Calories are the same in each—108 calories per tablespoon. Both are mainly fat.

Grapefruit breaks down body fat.
False. No food can do that. Grapefruit is, however a low-calorie food. One-half of a grapefruit is only 48 calories.

Calories to Eat

You know that food has energy, or calories. And you know that three nutrients provide calories. What are they? Carbohydrates and fat are the best energy sources. Protein provides calories, too. Protein foods are costly, so they are a more expensive way to get energy.

Almost every food has calories. But all foods don't have the same amount of calories. The number of calories depends on the amount of carbohydrate, fat, and protein in a food. Fat has more calories than carbohydrate and proteins do.

Foods with more calories are usually oily, greasy-crisp, sweet, or sticky. And foods with fewer calories are often watery-crisp, or puffed and airy.

There's a way to find the specific calorie amount in each food. Check a calorie chart. In these charts, calories are listed for foods in certain size servings. You can check a calorie chart to learn the calories in a snack. Or you can add up the calories you eat in one meal or one day.

WHICH SNACK IS FOR YOU?

Low-Calorie	High-Calorie
skim milk	milkshake
fruit juice	raisins
celery or carrot sticks	peanuts
green pepper	peanut butter sandwich
tomato	waffle
pickle	cheese
cantaloupe	watermelon slice
strawberries	ice cream
pear	
grapes	
plain bread slice	
saltines	

CALORIE CHART

Food	Amount	Calories	Food	Amount	Calories
Sour cream	¼ c	125	Potato (baked)	1	140
Cottage cheese	½ c	105	Potato chips	10	110
Milk (whole)	1 c	150	Tomatoes (raw)	1 raw	40
Milk (skim)	1 c	99	Mixed vegetables	1 c	120
Chocolate pudding	1 c	385	Potato salad	1 c	250
Ice cream	1 c	270	Apple (raw)	1	80
Ice milk	1 c	131	Applesauce	1 c	230
Yogurt (skim milk)	1 c	227	Bananas	1	100
Bacon	2 slices	90	Grapefruit	½	50
Hamburger (broiled)	3 oz	270	Strawberries (raw)	1 c	60
Beef and vegetable stew	1 c	220	Raisins	1 c	480
Ham	3 oz	159	Apple juice	1 c	120
Sausage	2 links	130	Orange juice	1 c	120
Frankfurter	1 frank	170	Bread, whole-wheat	1 slice	60
Chicken, fried	1 drumstick & 1 breast	250	Bread, enriched white	1 slice	70
Chicken, baked without skin	3 oz	160	Crackers, graham	2	50
Bologna	1 slice	80	Roll, hamburger	1 roll	80
Fish sticks	3	150	Cake, angelfood	1 slice	100
Tuna (packed in oil)	1 c	170	Cake, devil's food	1 slice	230
Tuna (packed in water)	1 c	110	Oatmeal	1 c	130
Egg (hard cooked)	1	80	Rice breakfast cereal	1 c	120
Egg (scrambled with milk and table fat)	1	90	Sugar cookies	4	140
Cashew nuts	1 c	790	Pancakes	2	120
Peanuts	1 c	840	Popcorn (without butter)	1 c	25
Macaroni and cheese	1 c	430	Cola	1 c	100
Pizza	1 slice	140	Butter/margarine	1 tbsp	100
Broccoli	1 stalk	45	Mayonnaise	1 tbsp	100
Brussels sprouts (cooked)	1 c	60	Catsup	1 tbsp	16
Carrots (cooked	1 c	50	Chicken noodle soup	1 c	60
Corn-on-the-cob	1 ear	70	Split-pea soup	1 c	140
Lettuce	1 c	8	Jelly	1 tbsp	50
			Syrup	1 tbsp	60
			White sugar	1 tbsp	40

Calories to Burn

Calories power everything your body does. Food contains calories. And the body burns those calories for energy. Movement burns calories. When you kick your legs, wave your hands, even wiggle your nose, your body uses calories. Body processes burn calories. Your breathing, your heart beat, and your digestion all use calories. You even burn calories when you sleep.

Some activities use more calories than others do. If you sit quietly, you use some calories. When you walk, you use more. And when you run, you use even more. The harder you work, the more calories you use. Which activity uses more calories—playing basketball or watching basketball? You're right if you said playing the game.

The longer you exercise, the more calories you burn, too. Again which activity uses more calories—swimming for ten minutes or for 20 minutes? The answer, of course, is 20 minutes.

CALORIES USED FOR ACTIVITIES

Type of Activity	Calories per hour
Sedentary	80 to 100
Activities done while sitting, with little or no arm movement. Reading; writing; eating; watching television or movies; sewing; playing cards.	
Light	110 to 160
Activities done while standing that require some arm movement, and strenuous activities done while sitting. Preparing food; doing dishes; dusting; handwashing small articles of clothing; ironing; walking slowly; personal care; rapid typing; filing in an office.	
Moderate	170 to 240
Activities done while standing that require moderate arm movement and activities done while sitting that require vigorous arm movement. Making beds, mopping, and scrubbing; sweeping; light polishing and waxing; laundering by machine; light gardening and carpentry work; walking moderately fast.	
Vigorous	250 to 350
Heavy scrubbing and waxing; handwashing large articles of clothing; hanging out clothes; walking fast; bowling; golfing; gardening.	
Strenuous	350 or more
Swimming; tennis; running; bicycling; dancing; skiing; football.	

USDA

HOW MANY CALORIES DO YOU NEED EACH DAY?

People need different amounts of calories. This shows the average amount that people your age need.

Boys begin their growth spurt later than girls do. Girls grow fastest between the ages of 11-14. Boys grow fastest from ages 15-18. That's why boys' calorie needs go up, and girls' calorie needs go down as they grow older.

Age	Girls	Boys
7-10	2400	2400
11-14	2200	2700
15-18	2100	2800

Source: 1980 Recommended Dietary Allowances

How Many Calories Do You Need?

Each person needs enough calories to power body processes and activities. The chart "How Many Calories Do You Need?" shows the average amount of calories people your age use daily. You might need more or less. Do you know why? People use up different amounts of calories in physical activity. Some people burn calories for their body processes faster than others do.

To keep your own best weight, the calories you eat should balance the calories you burn. Then you won't get fat and you won't lose weight either.

Diets That Work

Weight loss or gain takes time. Fat won't disappear overnight. And a skinny body won't take shape with a few big meals. On a good diet, people lose or gain about two pounds a week. A smart dieter is patient and follows a diet that makes sense. A doctor can help you develop a diet and exercise plan that's healthy. It should be a plan that you can stick to.

CUTTING THE FAT, CUTTING THE SUGAR

Fat and sugar provide calories. Cut calories in your diet by eating less of both!

Eat less fat.
- Trim fat off meat.
- Broil or bake food, instead of frying it.
- Skim fat off the top of gravy.
- Use less salad dressing.
- Use low-fat dairy products.
- Use plain yogurt instead of sour cream.
- Use less butter on bread, vegetables, and pasta.
- Use less fat and oil in cooking.

Eat less sugar.
- Drink water instead of soft drinks.
- Sweeten cereal with fruit, not sugar.
- Eat less candy and sweet desserts.
- Use fruit packed in water, not syrup.
- Use less sugar in cooking.

Trimming Down

Being a little overweight isn't a problem. Often pre-teenage pudginess or "baby fat" goes away with a little growing. Doctors do get concerned, however, when people have too much body fat.

Why do people get fat? Often it's because they eat more calories than their bodies burn, and the extra fuel is stored as body fat. That's the scientific reason. Why do some people eat more than they need?

- Certain moods cause some people to overeat. Do you ever eat when you're lonely, depressed, or bored?
- Some people eat without thinking. If food's around, they nibble.
- Some people are in the habit of eating too much. They have a hard time pushing themselves away from the dinner table.

Other people really don't overeat, they just under exercise! They get fat, too.

To lose weight, a person needs to eat fewer calories and use up more calories in exercise. Then the body has no extra energy to store as fat. Instead it uses up body fat already stored.

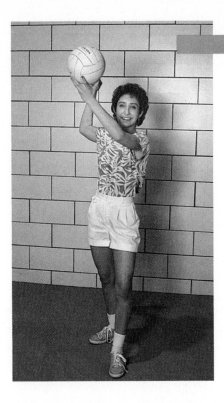

Exercise is just as important as eating habits for weight control and good health.

Eatng to Lose Weight   It isn't healthy to lose too much weight all at once. A person who needs to lose weight must learn to eat fewer calories. If you need to trim body fat, follow these tips for cutting down on calories:

- Eat a variety of low-calorie foods from the Daily Food Guide. Eat the recommended serving amounts. Keep foods from the Fats and Sweets Group to a minimum.
- Avoid second helpings.
- Eat slowly. Chew well. You won't eat as much. You might put your fork down between bites. Or make a mental game of trying to be the last one done eating—without eating a second helping!
- Serve less food on a smaller plate. It will look like more.
- Eat low-calorie snack foods.
- Drink water before a meal. Your appetite will be smaller.
- Fill up by eating more vegetables and salads. These are low-calorie foods if you don't add sauces and dressings.
- Eat foods with less fat and less sugar.

Eating habits can get in the way of weight loss. To lose weight more easily, remember:

- Don't skip meals! Meal skippers get hungry. They often eat more calories in snack foods than they would in a meal.
- If you're bored or upset, do something besides eat! Take a walk, enjoy a hobby, or talk to a friend.
- Watch out for times when you eat without thinking. Standing next to a bowl of chips is tempting! If you must nibble, stand next to a bowl of raw vegetables.
- Don't make excuses for cheating on your diet. In restaurants you can order low-calorie foods. And good friends understand if you refuse seconds.

Remember that foods themselves aren't fattening. But the amount you eat can be. If you're trying to lose weight, you can probably have a little bit of almost any food. Just be careful not to eat too much.

Exercise Burns Calories   The more active you are, the more calories you'll burn, and that makes weight loss easier. Exercise is an important part of weight loss.

One way to get exercise is to involve yourself in active sports. Find a sport you like. It may be one you can continue to enjoy as an adult. Skating, bicycling, swimming, and hiking use lots of calories.

Getting involved in active sports, is not the only way to get exercise. Another way to get exercise and burn more calories is to use more energy in everything you do.

- Use stairs instead of elevators.
- Find an active hobby instead of watching television.
- Walk when you talk with friends instead of sitting.

What other ways can you increase your activity?

Have your ever tempted a dieting friend with high-calorie snacks? Try to offer nutritious, low-calorie snacks next time.

Getting involved in active sports is one way to get exercise.

Shaping Up

Did you ever hear someone say, "I'm too skinny"? Since so many people try hard to lose weight, we forget that others wish they could gain some.

There are several reasons why people are thin. Some people in their early teens grow so fast that their bodies put calories into growing and not into padding. Eventually, they'll get a nice shape when their growth stops.

Other people are thin because they don't eat enough. Maybe they're too excited or "wound-up" at mealtimes. Or maybe they're overactive. They burn up more calories than they take in.

Still other thin people come from families who are thin. They seem to burn up every calorie no matter how much they eat!

Eating to Gain Weight   It is hard for some people to gain weight. To gain, they need to eat more calories than they burn. If you want to gain weight, these are ways to add calories to your food choices:

- Eat a variety of higher-calorie foods from the Daily Food Guide. Eat the recommended serving amounts plus a little more.
- Enjoy second helpings.
- Eat higher-calorie snack foods. Don't eat too many empty-calorie foods.

Some people need to change their habits in order to gain weight. Here are some ways this can be done:

- If you have a small appetite, eat six small meals instead of three larger meals.
- Don't skip meals.
- If necessary, relax 15 minutes before mealtime. Then you won't be too excited to eat.
- If you rush around a lot, maybe you need to take time to relax a little and then eat.

There's a note of caution, however. When teens are growing, they sometimes eat and eat to gain weight. They should watch how much they gain because teenagers who get fat might have a hard time taking extra weight off when they get older.

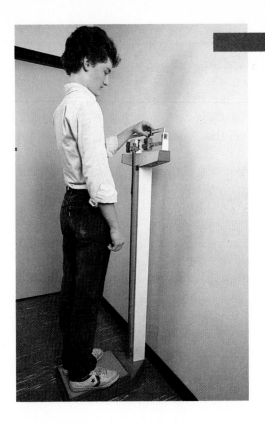

Don't give up if the scale doesn't rise or drop quickly enough for you. Weight loss or weight gain doesn't always show up right away, but it will if you stick with a proper diet and exercise plan.

Exercise Builds Muscles   Exercise can sometimes add shape and curves to the body. That's because exercise builds muscles. Muscle gives the body its shape.

Both boys and girls get stronger when they exercise. Both build their muscles, however, boys can increase their muscle size more than girls can. Remember that exercise also burns calories. People who increase exercise to build muscles also need to eat more.

Diets That Don't Work

Losing or gaining weight takes time. But sometimes people are impatient. They want quick results, often with little work. And so they try one fad diet after another. Usually, these diets just don't work—at least not for long!

What Is a Fad Diet?

A fad is something that is immensely popular for a short period of time and then everybody quickly loses interest because it becomes "old," boring, or is just not the great thing it promised to be. A *fad diet* is a special diet for losing weight which becomes very popular because it promises easy methods for quickly losing weight. People don't stick to these diets very long because they soon find that the diet just isn't the "miracle" cure for their weight problem.

Fad diets usually don't work. At least, they don't control weight for long because most people can't stay on them very long. Also, they do not help people learn new eating habits. Often they go back to old eating habits. So body fat goes right back on.

Other fad diets make phoney promises. These diets can make you sick if you follow them for a while. Being a little heavy is better than letting a fad diet make you sick. Fad diets often don't have all the nutrients people need. And so they make people tired and irritable. People who follow these diets don't have the energy for school and other activities. Worse yet, they don't get the nutrients needed for growth and health.

ON SCENE ...

January 14   GREATEST PAPER EVER

Why Ian Strong has the strength
of steel . . . . Page 5

Dinah Myte talks frankly about her
beauty secrets . . . . Page 9

50¢

"All-You-Can-Eat Zucchini Diet"

DOCTOR ANNOUNCES BREAKTHROUGH IN WEIGHT LOSS

Dr. Byrde Seed, a well-known plant expert, just announced a breakthrough in weight loss. According to Dr. Seed, the new "All-You-Can-Eat Zucchini Diet" is guaranteed to promote weight loss within the first week.

In a recent book, Dr. Seed outlines simple steps to weight loss through the zucchini diet. A strict menu plan provides an easy guideline for food choices. The book discusses the health benefits of zucchini and gives many delicious recipes for preparing zucchini at home.

Dr. Seed has done extensive research on zucchini and other types of squash. Without question, the zucchini diet will take off pounds while satisfying the appetite.

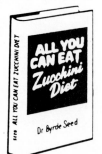

MENU PLAN

Breakfast
Raw zucchini—unlimited amount—25 cal. per 1/2 c.
Skim milk—8 oz.—88 cal.
Toast—1 slice, unbuttered—61 cal.

Lunch
Hard-cooked egg—1—82 cal.
Zucchini-vegetable soup—1 c.—50 cal.
Saltines—2—24 cal.

Dinner
Boiled or broiled zucchini—unlimited amount—25 cal. per 1/2 c.
Broiled lean meat, poultry, or fish—3 oz.—185 cal.
Rice—1/2 c. unbuttered—112 cal.
Skim milk—8 oz.—88 cal.

Snacks
Raw zucchini—unlimited amount—25 cal. per 1/2 c.

How Can You Judge a Diet?

Magazines and books have so many diets to choose from. Assume for a moment that you want to lose weight. How do you know which diet to follow? How do you know which one is good for you? Ask yourself these questions before you start:

- Does it follow the Daily Food Guide? Only a balanced diet has all the nutrients you need to stay healthy.
- Does it tell you to eat a variety of foods, not just a few? Some diets tell you to concentrate on a single food, such as grapefruit, bananas, or rice. But it takes many different foods to provide the nutrients you need to grow and stay healthy. Besides, you can't stick to a single-food diet for long. The food soon becomes boring and unappetizing.
- Does it provide at least 1400 calories a day? You need enough calories for your body to work and grow in a healthy way. The Daily Food Guide recommendations can provide that many calories if foods from the Fats and Sweets Group are avoided.
- Does it look and taste good? You probably won't eat food you don't like for very long.
- Does it require vitamin pills? A good diet relies on nutritious foods, not pills!
- Does it fit your lifestyle? If the answer is "no," you won't follow the diet for long. For example, a diet that requires clear soup every day at 10:30 am is impossible when you're in school!
- Do you need to buy something to make the diet work? If so, the diet may be nonsense. And it may waste your money.
- Does it match your budget? You can't stay on a diet long if the foods cost too much.
- Is the person who wrote the diet qualified? Sometimes this question is hard to answer. Ask your home economics teacher, the school nurse, or your doctor about the diet.
- Does it teach you a new way to eat? People who overeat need to learn new eating habits. In that way, they won't overeat again when the diet is over!

Look at the "All-You-Can-Eat Zucchini Diet." How would you judge this diet?

Danger—Losing Too Much Weight!

Television and magazines keep telling us that "looks are everything" or that "thin is in." Some people get so obsessed by this message that they lose too much weight! No matter how thin they are, they still think they're fat.

People with this extreme desire to be thin might have *anorexia.* They starve themselves until they look almost like a skeleton. And they hardly have enough energy to move. They may even need hospital care and feeding so they don't die.

Others who become overly worried about their weight may develop *bulimia.* People with bulimia go on eating binges in which they eat way too much. Then they make themselves vomit to get rid of the food they just ate so they won't gain any weight. This is very dangerous to health, too.

Usually, these problems are bigger than wanting to be slim. People with anorexia or bulimia don't feel good about themselves. But they won't admit it, even to themselves. Maybe they don't get along with their parents. Maybe they want their parents to suffer, too. People with these problems need a doctor's care to get well.

Planning a Weight Control Diet

Now you know about calories and you know that people can control their weight by eating fewer calories or more calories than their bodies use. You also know what makes a healthy diet. With a small group of students in class, plan a day's food choices for these two people:

- Chris wants to lose six pounds. She can eat 1400 calories a day and probably lose two pounds a week.
- Mark wants to gain six pounds. He can eat 3700 calories a day and probably gain two pounds a week.

Choose three meals and snacks for each one for one day. Be sure to follow the guidelines of the Daily Food Guide. Make a list of tips for both Chris and Mark that will help them meet their weight goals. Remind them to exercise!

Whether you plan food choices for Chris, Mark, or yourself, remember the key to weight control is the number of calories eaten and the number of calories used for energy. Then keep your own best weight by choosing a nutritious and sensible diet from the Daily Food Guide.

CHAPTER REVIEW

Summary

Each person has a body weight that's best. A pinch test is a rough estimate of body fat, but a doctor should recommend the best weight for someone.

Calories measure the energy in food and the energy people need. The body needs calories for body processes and exercise. Some people use more calories than others do.

You control weight through food choices and exercise. People may need to change the foods they eat and their eating habits to gain or lose weight. Fad diets often promise quick weight loss. They usually don't help a person reach a weight goal permanently. Most aren't nutritionally balanced, and so they may be harmful to health.

What Have You Learned?

1. Why is weight control important?
2. How does the body use calories?
3. Name ten high-calorie foods. Name ten low-calorie foods.
4. What are five ways to eat fewer calories? What are five ways to eat more calories?
5. How can exercise help you control your weight?
6. Why can fad diets be harmful?
7. How can you judge a diet?
8. What is anorexia? Bulimia?

Things to Do

1. Find a calorie chart. Add up the calories in one day's food choices. Be sure to include your snacks.
2. Keep an exercise diary. Write down all the ways you include activity in your daily life.
3. Make snack posters. One should show high-calorie, nutritious snack foods. The other should show low-calorie, nutritious snack foods.
4. Find a weight gain or weight loss diet in a magazine. Judge the diet using guidelines in this chapter.

GETTING READY TO COOK

appliances	food preparation equipment that uses gas or electricity
beat	to mix ingredients quickly until smooth
ingredients	specific foods that are part of a recipe
level off	to fill the measuring cup or spoon beyond the top, then use a spatula to scrape off the excess
measure	to determine a specific amount
recipe	a list of ingredients and the directions for putting them together
stir	to use a spoon to mix slowly in a circular motion
utensils	small pieces of kitchen equipment used for food preparation and serving
whip	to mix or beat very fast to add air and volume to the mixture

CHAPTER 5

After reading this chapter, you should be able to:

- *follow a simple recipe.*
- *measure dry and liquid ingredients accurately.*
- *describe the use and care of various kitchen utensils.*
- *describe the use and care of three kitchen appliances.*
- *state two ways to save household energy in the kitchen.*

A re you ready to cook? Some people think that being a good cook is just luck, that cooking comes naturally to some and not others. That isn't true.

You have to learn to use recipes and kitchen equipment to be a good cook. You also need to learn to measure accurately. Cooking is fun when you know how!

There are many cookbooks and recipes to choose from. Before purchasing a cookbook look at it closely to determine if you can follow the directions and if the ingredients are familiar to you.

Using Recipes

A *recipe* is a set of food preparation instructions. First, it tells what ingredients you need and how much of each ingredient will be used. Then it tells how to combine them. *Ingredients* are specific foods that make up a recipe. For example, cheese and sausage are two ingredients in a pizza recipe.

A recipe acts as a planning guide. It tells the kind and size of utensils you need. For example, do you need a small or a large saucepan? It also tells the number of servings it will make. Then you know if the recipe feeds just one person or a group of four or even more. It tells the cooking temperature and how long a food needs to cook. Then you know if you have enough time to prepare the food.

Reading a Recipe

Recipes are like road maps. Some are more complicated than others. You must follow them carefully to be successful:

- Read the recipe carefully. Look up words you don't know.
- Gather all the utensils you need. Organize them so you can prepare food easily.
- Gather all the ingredients you need. Put them on a tray. When the tray is empty, you know you have used all the ingredients.
- Measure carefully.
- Follow the directions in a step-by-step order.

The Words in Recipes

Recipes use a special language. It's not a foreign language from a far-away place. In fact, you know most of the words already. But in cooking, the words take on a special meaning. As an example, let's look at some of the words for mixing.

- The word *stir* means to use a spoon to mix slowly in a circular motion. You stir soup or a sauce.
- You *beat* the ingredients in a cookie recipe. This means to mix them quickly with a spoon or an electric mixer. The ingredients turn over and over until they're completely blended.
- To *whip*, you mix very fast to add air to the mixture. This increases the amount, or the volume, of the mixture.

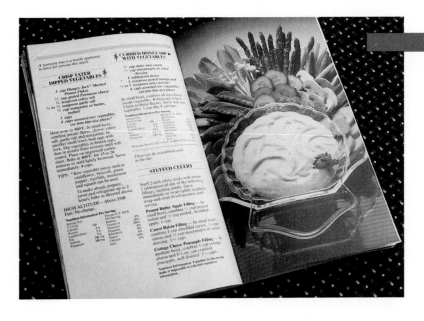

Recipes come in many different formats. Those that list ingredients first, then step-by-step directions are the easiest to follow.

WHAT DO THESE RECIPE WORDS MEAN?

Bake	To cook by dry heat in an oven
Baste	To moisten with melted butter, cooking liquid, or other liquids while food roasts or bakes
Beat	To mix quickly until smooth
Blend	To mix two or more ingredients completely
Boil	To cook liquids at a high temperature where bubbles rise and break
Braise	To cook in a small amount of liquid in a covered pan
Broil	To cook by direct heat, such as grilling
Chop	To cut into small pieces with a knife or other utensil
Cream	To mix until soft and smooth
Dice	To chop into very small pieces
Drain	To remove liquid from food by pouring off the liquid from the food, placing the food in a sieve or colander, or by placing the food on paper towels to absorb the liquid
Fry	To cook in fat, usually in a frying pan
Grate	To shred into small pieces
Grease	To rub with fat or oil
Mash	To make soft and smooth by crushing or beating
Melt	To change a solid to a liquid with heat
Pare	To cut or pull off the peel
Roast	To cook uncovered in an oven
Saute	To fry lightly and quickly
Season	To add spices or herbs to change the flavor of food
Simmer	To cook in a liquid, just below the boiling point
Steam	To cook, covered, over boiling water
Stew	To simmer in liquid
Stir	To mix with a slow, circular motion
Stir fry	To cook thinly-sliced food fast in a small amount of hot fat
Strain	To remove liquid from a food using a utensil with holes

Measuring Ingredients

To *measure* is to determine the specific amount of something. Measuring correctly is very important. If you don't use the right amount of each ingredient, the recipe probably won't turn out right.

Measuring cups and spoons help you measure exactly. Measuring in a drinking cup just won't give good results.

Recipes often abbreviate amounts. Abbreviate means to shorten. These are some abbreviations you'll see in recipes:

- t. and tsp. mean teaspoon
- T. and tbsp. mean tablespoon
- c. means cup
- f.g. means few grains. This means a very small amount, such as the amount of salt you can hold between your thumb and first finger.

Some recipes call for a dash. A dash is also a small amount. Generally, it's less than ⅛ teaspoon.

Measuring Dry Ingredients   There are two kinds of measuring cups. One type is for dry ingredients, such as flour. You fill the cup. Then you level off the ingredient with a spatula. To *level off*, you fill the measuring cup as full as possible then scrape a spatula across the top to make certain the measuring cup is completely full. These cups aren't good for measuring liquids. They're too easy to spill. Measuring cups for dry ingredients come in different sizes: 1 cup, ½ cup, ⅓ cup, and ¼ cup. A set of dry measuring cups has one of each size. Amounts smaller than ¼ cup are measured in measuring spoons.

Dry measuring cups come in sets, are used to measure one amount and must be filled to the top, then leveled off with a spatula.

A liquid measuring cup can measure different amounts, has a lip for easy pouring, and extra space at the top to avoid spills.

Measuring Liquid Ingredients   Liquids are measured in clear glass or plastic cups. A 1-cup measuring cup is marked to show the level for ¼ cup, ⅓ cup, ½ cup, ⅔ cup, ¾ cup, and 1 cup. To measure, place the cup on a flat surface. Fill the cup until the liquid reaches the correct line. Check the amount at eye level without picking up the cup. Remember that glass measuring cups are breakable!

Both liquid and dry ingredients are measured in measuring spoons. They come in different sizes—usually 1 tablespoon, 1 teaspoon, ½ teaspoon and ¼ teaspoon to a set.

Using Kitchen Equipment

Utensils are pieces of kitchen equipment. Some utensils are used to prepare food. Others are used for serving. Can you name the utensils in your kitchen? What do these utensils do?

Small Utensils

A carpenter has workroom tools, such as screwdrivers and hammers. To prepare food, you have kitchen tools, or utensils, for doing specific jobs in food preparation. Some do just one job, while others can do several.

Small utensils are used for cutting and spreading, mixing, stirring, or blending, chopping, mashing, or crushing, draining or straining, lifting or turning, and measuring.

The chart on pages 89–92 shows common kitchen utensils with their names. It also lists specific jobs for each one.

KITCHEN UTENSILS HAVE SPECIFIC JOBS

Use	Utensil	Specific Job
Cutting and Spreading	Bread knife	Cut bread or sandwiches. Slice cheese.
	Carving knife	Cut meat, such as roast beef or pork.
	Kitchen shears	Trim vegetables. Cut apart poultry. Snip parsley.
	Paring knife	Remove peels from fruits and vegetables. Cut fruits and small vegetables.
	Pizza cutter	Cut pizza slices. Cut rolled cookies or pastry.
	Serrated knife	Cut around the sections of fruit, such as grapefruit. A grapefruit knife is serrated with a curved tip. Slice tomatoes
	Spatula	Spread sandwich filling, cream cheese, or frosting. Level off dry ingredients, such as flour, when measuring them. Lift rolls or cookies from a pan. Loosen bread and other foods from a pan.
	Utility knife	Cut or slice fruit, vegetables, small meat, and pies.
	Vegetable peeler	Remove the skins from some fruits and vegetables. Some peelers can be used to core apples.

Bread Knife

Carving Knife

Kitchen Shears

Paring Knife

Pizza Cutter

(Continued on next page)

Serrated Knife

Spatula

Utility Knife

Vegetable Peeler

Use	Utensil	Specific Job
Mixing, Stirring, and Blending	Pastry blender	Blend butter or margarine into flour mixtures for pies, biscuits, and some yeast breads.
	Rubber scraper	Mix or stir food in a bowl. Remove food from containers.
	Metal spoon	Mix or stir food in a bowl. Metal spoons should be used in a pot or pan only if they have wood or plastic handles because the metal gets hot and can burn you.
	Wire whisk	Whip, blend, cream, beat eggs, and whip cream. It puts air into the mixture.
	Wooden spoon	Mix or stir food in a hot pot or pan, perhaps as food cooks. A wooden spoon doesn't get hot as a metal spoon does, and it doesn't scratch non-stick pans. Mix or stir ingredients in a bowl. Wooden spoons shouldn't soak in water or they will split.

Pastry Blender

Rubber Scraper

Metal Spoon

(Continued on next page)

Wire Whisk

Potato Masher

Rolling Pin

Shredder Grater

Wooden Spoon

Slotted Spoon

Strainer

KITCHEN UTENSILS HAVE SPECIFIC JOBS (Continued)

Use	Utensil	Specific Job
Chopping, Mashing, and Crushing	Potato masher	Mash potatoes or turnips. Mash fruit for jam.
	Rolling pin	Make bread and cracker crumbs. Roll out dough for pastry, cookies, and biscuits.
	Shredder grater	Shred vegetables, lettuce, and cheese. Grate cheese, citrus peel, and chocolate.
Draining and Straining	Slotted spoon	Remove vegetables and other foods from liquids.
	Strainer	Wash fruit and vegetables. Drain pasta. Crumble hard-cooked egg yolks for salads.
Dipping, Lifting, or Turning	Ladle	Spoon out soups and stews.
	Long-handled fork	Turn pan-fried foods. Turn foods in a flour or bread crumb mixture. Hold meat or poultry while slicing.
	Melon baller	Make fruit balls from melons and other soft fruit. Make cheese or butter balls.
	Scoop	Serve rounded, equal portions of cottage cheese, ice cream, rice, or mashed potatoes.

(Continued on next page)

Ladle

Long-handled Fork

Melon Baller   **Scoop**

KITCHEN UTENSILS HAVE SPECIFIC JOBS (Continued)

Use	Utensil	Specific Job
Dipping, Lifting, or Turning (Continued) **Turner**	Turner	Turn foods in a frying pan. Remove foods from a frying pan or cookie sheet. Serve quiche, cake, or pie.
	Tongs	Remove food, such as corn-on-the-cob, from hot liquids. Turn food on a broiler or grill.
Measuring **Dry Measures**	Dry measures	Measure dry ingredients. Measuring cups that need to be leveled off. Measure 1-cup, ½ cup, ⅓ cup, ¼ cup.
	Liquid measuring cup	Measure liquid ingredients. A one-cup measure is marked to show the level for 1 cup, ½ cup, ⅓ cup and ¼ cup.
	Measuring spoons	Measure small amounts of dry and liquid ingredients: 1 tablespoon, 1 teaspoon, ½ teaspoon, ¼ teaspoon.
Doing Other Jobs	Can opener	Open canned foods.
	Pastry brush	Baste meat and poultry with a sauce. Brush vegetables with sauce. Brush frosting on cookies.
	Small skewers	Hold together stuffed fish or poultry. Hold together rolled roast or stuffed chops.
	Vegetable brush	Clean fresh fruit and vegetables.

Tongs

Liquid Measuring Cup

Measuring Spoons

Can Opener

Pastry Brush

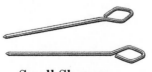

Small Skewers

Vegetable Brush

Utensils for Cooking

Many foods are heated or cooked in pots and pans. What determines which pot or pan to use? First, you decide what you'll cook. Will you make a cake or a pie? Each one uses a different kind of pan.

Then you decide how you'll cook the food. Will you fry or simmer it? Or will you bake it in the oven? Then you choose a pot or pan which is the right size. The chart on page 92 shows several different pots and pans. It describes how to use each one.

Using Pots and Pans

What else should you know about pots and pans?

- Pots are sometimes called saucepans.
- Cover a pot when you are boiling or simmering. You often cover food in the oven, too. Food in a covered pot cooks faster.
- In a double boiler, put water in the bottom. The food goes in the pan which fits on top. To cook, be sure you have enough water in the bottom. The water should not touch the top pan.
- Don't fill pans too full or they'll run over when heated. They're also hard to handle without spilling if they are too full. Use a larger pan if you have to.
- To prevent accidents, keep the handles of pots and pans turned toward the center of the range. Don't let the handles stick out over another burner. If the other burner accidentally gets turned on, the handle of the pan will become hot and may even melt or begin to burn. Don't let handles hang over the edge of the range because they may get bumped and the pan may spill.
- Metal spoons damage pots and pans with nonstick finishes. Use wooden or plastic utensils.
- Some pans, handles, and lids get very hot. Use a potholder to remove lids and hold handles so you won't get burned.
- If food burns in a pan, let the pan cool before you add water. Otherwise, water might splatter in your face. Cold water can also warp a very hot pan. A warped pan doesn't have a flat bottom. Warped pans are dangerous because they tip over more easily.
- Clean pots and pans after they cool down. Some can be cleaned with a pot scrubber. But use a soft dishcloth and soapy water to clean nonstick finishes because metal scrubbers damage the surface. Plastic scrubbers work well on nonstick surfaces.

COOKING UTENSILS: HOW TO USE THEM

Baking Pan

Casserole Dish

Cookie Sheet

Double Boiler

Baking pan	Bake fish, vegetables, or desserts. Roast meat or poultry.
Casserole dish	Bake mistures of food, such as vegetables or meat, in the oven.
Cookie sheet	Bake cookies and rolls.
Cooling rack	Cool hot foods.
Double boiler	Keep food away from the direct heat of the stove's burner. It is used for cooking custards and melting chocolate.
Frypan	Fry foods in a small amount of fat. Fry bacon or scrambled eggs. Cook pancakes.
Muffin tin	Bake muffins or cupcakes in the oven.
Saucepan	Heat or cook a small amount of food.
Sauce pot	Cook a large amount of food. Cook food that needs a lot of water, such as noodles or rice. Make stew or soup. Cook corn-on-the-cob or lobster.
Teakettle	Heat water for any purpose.
Vegetable steamer	Cook vegetables above boiling water.
Wok	Steam foods. Stir-fry vegetables.

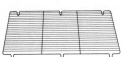

Cooling Rack

Muffin Tin

Sauce Pot

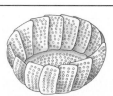

Vegetable Steamer

Frypan

Saucepan

Teakettle

Wok

Other Equipment

A well-equipped kitchen has other equipment, too. Think for a moment. What else is in your kitchen at home or in the home economics department?

Mixing Bowls Mixing bowls are made of aluminum, plastic, or glass. They come in all sizes—small, medium, and large. The right bowl is one that's big enough to hold the ingredients without having them spill over while you mix.

Cutting Boards Cutting boards have a wood or a hard plastic surface for cutting, slicing, and chopping. The board protects both knives and countertops.

Potholders Potholders are cloth pads used to hold hot utensils and to protect counter tops. They keep your hands and the counter from getting burned.

Timer A timer helps you remember how long a food has cooked. You set the time and a sound goes off when the time is up.

Wire Racks A wire rack is a rack used to keep hot pans off counter and table tops. They are also used to cool cakes and cookies. Some racks are used in roaster pans to hold meat and poultry up out of the juice while cooking.

As you learn more about cooking, you'll learn to use other utensils, too.

Mixing bowls come in many sizes and can be metal, plastic or glass. When selecting one be sure it's large enough to hold all your ingredients and allow for mixing.

Appliances

Appliances are types of food preparation equipment that run by gas or electricity. Gas and electricity are often called household energy. Small appliances include a toaster, food processor, popcorn popper, and coffeemaker. The range, microwave oven, refrigerator, and dishwasher are large appliances. Stores refer to large appliances as major appliances.

Small Appliances   Small appliances save personal energy. Personal energy is the effort you use to do a job. A food processor helps you chop or slice foods. An electric mixer might whip cream or mix the ingredients for a cake. If the job is very small, it may be faster to mix by hand.

Some small appliances also cook foods. A toaster-oven and a slow cooker are two examples. You might save electricity by using small appliances. For example, you use less household energy to bake a small piece of fish in a toaster-oven. A large oven would take more household energy because it's heating up a larger space.

Can you name some other small appliances? A blender, an electric knife, and a waffle iron are three more examples.

Many small appliances are available. Before you purchase be sure you will use it enough to justify the cost. Also be sure you have room to store it.

Large Appliances   Large appliances help you do the major tasks in the kitchen. A range, a microwave oven, a refrigerator, and a dishwasher are large appliances.

Range   A range, either gas or electric, cooks for you. It has burners on the top surface and one or two ovens. A range transfers heat to a pan and then food gets heated or cooked. Metal pots and pans are most commonly used to cook food on a range. A range is often called a stove.

What special tips should you remember about a range?

- Wipe up spills each time you cook, and thoroughly clean the range each week.
- Arrange oven shelves before you turn on the heat. Then you won't burn yourself.
- Arrange pans in the oven so they don't touch each other. Hot air must move around them.
- Don't leave burners on when you aren't cooking. It's dangerous! A range should never be used to heat a room.

BE ENERGY WISE

Household energy is expensive. Good cooks don't waste it. These are some ways you can be energy wise!

Range
- Keep the oven door closed so hot air won't escape.
- Use lids on pots and pans, when appropriate, to keep the heat in.
- Trim the flame. It should be no bigger than the pot.

Refrigerator
- Keep the freezer compartment full. Then there's less cold air to escape.
- Don't pack the refrigerator compartment too full. The cool air needs to move around the food.
- Defrost the freezer regularly to get rid of the ice which forms. A freezer must work harder, using more energy, when ice builds up. Some refrigerators defrost themselves.
- Keep the door closed unless you're getting something. Keep cold air in and warm air out.

Dishwasher
- Fill the dishwasher with dishes before you turn it on. It uses the same amount of hot water and energy for a small load as it does for a large load, so wait until you have a full load of dishes before you use it.

Microwave Oven   A microwave oven is another major appliance. For small amounts of food, it cooks much faster than a range. And it uses less household energy too. Metal cooking utensils damage a microwave oven. Instead, use glass, paper, or plastic wrap. Never start a microwave oven if it's empty!

Refrigerator   Refrigerators keep food cold. Most refrigerators also have a freezer compartment. Remember to clean the refrigerator each week and throw away spoiled food.

Dishwasher   Many kitchens have dishwashers, too. They aren't necessary, but they can save time and personal energy. You may even use less water than you use when doing dishes by hand. If you wash dishes in a dishwasher, use dishwasher detergent and not dish detergent.

Microwave ovens can save you a lot of time. They cook small quantities of food in a fraction of the time it takes to cook on a range or in an oven.

Practice for Measuring

Practice makes perfect! Find the measuring utensils in your kitchen. Then practice your measuring skills as you make two nutritious snacks—Trail Mix and Fruit Cooler. The recipes are on pages 99 and 100 of this chapter. The recipes are for four servings. How would you change the measurements to feed two people? Eight people?

Measuring Ingredients for Trail Mix

The ingredients in the Trail Mix are all dry ingredients. What measuring utensils will you need? You're right if you said four dry measures—1 cup, ½ cup, ¼ cup, and 1 tablespoon.

What is the right way to measure dry ingredients? Remember that you fill the ingredients to the top. Then you level off the top with a knife or spatula.

The ingredients are mixed in a bowl. What size bowl would be good to use? A small bowl that holds three to four cups is fine. Do you know why?

TRAIL MIX

Ingredients

1 cup granola
½ cup peanuts
¼ cup raisins
2 tablespoons sunflower seeds

Directions
1. Using the dry measuring cups, measure granola, peanuts, and raisins into a bowl.
2. Using the measuring spoons, measure sunflower seeds. Add to the mixture in the bowl.
3. Stir ingredients with a spoon until blended.

Yield: four ½-cup servings

Measuring Ingredients for Fruit Cooler

The ingredients in the Fruit Cooler are liquids. What measuring utensils will you need? You're right if you said a 1 cup liquid measure and 1 tablespoon. Why can you use the same mixing bowl for the Fruit Cooler that you used for the Trail Mix?

Getting ready to cook means knowing about recipes and about kitchen equipment. Now you're ready.

FRUIT COOLER

Ingredients

1 cup orange juice
¾ cup cranberry juice cocktail
⅓ cup ginger ale
1 tablespoon lemon juice

Directions

1. Using a liquid measuring cup, measure orange juice, cranberry juice, and ginger ale into a pitcher.
2. Using measuring spoons, measure lemon juice. Add to the ingredients in the pitcher.
3. Blend with a mixing spoon.

Yield: four ½-cup servings

CHAPTER REVIEW

Summary

Following a recipe carefully and measuring correctly help the recipe turn out right. Dry and liquid ingredients are measured in different ways.

Knowing the names of kitchen utensils, what they look like, and how they are used is part of being a good cook.

Kitchen appliances use electricity and gas. Small appliances, such as mixers, save time and personal energy. Large appliances such as a range, microwave oven, refrigerator, and dishwasher, help with the big jobs. A good cook knows how to save household energy when using appliances.

What Have You Learned?

1. What does a recipe tell you?
2. What is the correct way to measure one cup of flour? One cup of milk?
3. Why is measuring correctly so important?
4. Name five small utensils, and tell how you could use each one.
5. What are three tips for using pots and pans?
6. Name five small appliances in your kitchen at school or at home, and describe what they do.
7. What are three tips for using a range?
8. What kind of utensils should you use in a microwave oven?
9. Describe two ways you can save household energy in the kitchen.

Things to Do

1. Go to a drawer in the foods lab. Take out one kitchen utensil you can't call by name, or choose one you don't know how to use. Hold it up in front of the class. Does anyone in the class know how it is used? If not, the teacher can tell you.
2. Choose one or two cooking terms from the list on page 86. Show the class how to do this food preparation step.
3. Make an energy-saver poster to hang in your foods lab. It might tell about household energy or personal energy.

LET'S COOK

dovetail	to accomplish more than one task at the same time
evaluate	to judge something
germ	living things too small to see with the eye alone that may spread illness
foods lab	kitchen in the classroom
manage	to use resources wisely
resource	any person or anything that helps you do what you want to

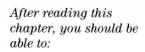

After reading this chapter, you should be able to:

- *list steps for preparing food in the kitchen.*
- *make a plan for preparing food in the school lab.*
- *provide tips for proper kitchen clean up at home and at school.*
- *state ways to keep food clean and safe to eat.*
- *identify ways to avoid accidents in the kitchen.*

T ime and personal energy are two of your most precious resources. A *resource* is something that can help you accomplish what you set out to do. Money is a resource too. Generally, resources are limited. You only have 24 hours in a day, and probably less than one hour to cook in class! Money is almost always limited. Good management is part of being a good cook. To *manage* is to use resources wisely. Follow these guidelines for wise management.

- Plan ahead. Answer these questions. What foods will I serve? What recipe should I follow? What food and equipment do I need? How many people will eat? How much cooking time do I have?
- Write a menu plan that considers your resources.
- Give yourself enough time to cook. When you serve more people, it usually takes longer. You have more food to prepare. For example, suppose you prepare a half grapefruit for breakfast. If it takes one minute to make one serving, how long will it take to make four servings? When time and energy are in short supply, choose recipes that you can prepare fast. For example, you can make scrambled eggs for four almost as fast as for one person. Some cooking procedures are faster, too. Broiling is faster than braising.

The food you prepare uses your time, energy, and money. Prepare only as much as people will eat.

Don't paint yourself into a corner by giving yourself an impossible task. Cooking takes time. Be sure to plan accordingly.

Cleaning up is an important part of cooking.

Cooking at Home

After you've planned your meal or snack, chosen your recipes, and done your shopping, you're ready to cook. There are several steps in preparing a meal. First, you take out the ingredients and equipment. Next, you prepare the food. And last, you clean up.

Gathering Ingredients and Equipment

Recipes list all the ingredients you need. Check to see that you have everything before you start preparing the food. In fact, get the ingredients out so they're handy. Then you can cook without being interrupted.

Do you have the equipment the recipe requires? Some recipes require a certain size pan. Use the type and size equipment the recipe calls for so it will come out right. Before you start preparing food, arrange all the equipment on the counter where you'll work.

Preparing Food

For good results, prepare food according to the directions. Save time and energy by managing your kitchen tasks well.

Following Directions   Recipes must be followed in step-by-step order. Otherwise, a step might be forgotten! Then the recipe won't turn out as you expect.

Measuring carefully is a must. Use the correct equipment. If necessary, read about measuring again in chapter 5. The cooking terms in a recipe have special meaning. Look them up if necessary. For example, do you know the difference between:

- bake and broil? Both are ways to cook inside the oven. To bake is to cook by dry, indirect heat. To broil is to cook by dry direct heat, such as to grill. Broiling requires a higher temperature.
- boil and simmer? Both are ways to cook liquids on a burner. Boiling is to cook liquids at a high temperature where bubbles rise and break. Simmering is cooking liquids just below the boiling point, when bubbles just begin to appear at the edge of the pan.
- pan fry and deep-fat fry? Both are cooking in hot fat or oil. To pan fry, you cook in a small amount of fat or oil. And to deep-fat fry, you cook in fat or oil that is deep enough for the food to float in it.

A recipe tells the length of cooking time. Use a timer to remind you when the cooking time is up. Don't guess. The food might burn, or it might not be done.

Working Ahead   Many foods need some preparation before they can be used in a recipe. Fresh fruits and vegetables need to be washed. Maybe they need to be chopped or sliced, too. You may need to cook rice or noodles. Meat may require browning. These are called pre-preparation steps.

One way to save food preparation time is to do some pre-preparation steps ahead. The night before, you might grate cheese for pizza. Or you could shape hamburgers into patties. Then wrap the food you have pre-prepared tightly, or put it in a tightly closed container and place it in the refrigerator.

Dovetailing   Dovetailing food preparation steps is a way to be efficient. To *dovetail* is to accomplish more than one task at the same time. For example, while water boils for cooking noodles, you make a salad.

Any pre-preparation you can do ahead of time will save you cooking time.

Cleaning Up

Clean up is a food preparation step. The kitchen should be clean and tidy when a meal is over.

Cleaning Efficiently Clean up doesn't start when the meal is over. Efficient cooks clean up as they work. That makes the job faster and easier at the end of the meal. Working in a tidy kitchen is more pleasant and often faster, too. These are some clean-up tasks you can do as you prepare a meal:

- Fill the sink with hot, soapy water. As you finish with utensils, let them soak. Remember wooden spoons shouldn't soak. Don't put knives in a sink full of soapy water, or you may reach into the water and cut yourself.
- Wipe the counter when you're done with a task. Put away unused ingredients when you're finished with them so you'll have more work space for the next task.
- Wash preparation dishes as you wait for food to cook.
- After you serve the food on plates or in bowls, put the pots and pans in soapy water to soak. Then they'll be easier to wash after you eat.

Putting supplies away when you're finished with them helps to keep your work area clean and makes the final clean up a lot easier.

Washing Dishes   There are several steps in washing dishes:

- Scrape left over food from the dishes into the garbage pail or the disposer. A garbage disposer is an appliance in the sink that grinds garbage. If you have a disposer in your classroom kitchen, have your teacher show you how to use it. Bones, pits, foil, and paper can't be put in the disposer.
- Wash glasses, dishes, flatware, and utensils in hot, soapy water.
- Rinse with hot water.
- Dry dishes with a clean towel or let them air dry.
- Put dishes away in cabinets or drawers so they stay clean.

If you have a dishwasher, scrape and rinse dishes and flatware first. Then load them into the dishwasher.

Cooking in the School Lab

Cooking at school is somewhat different from cooking at home. At home, you may be the only one cooking. But at school, you cook as part of a group. At home you may have plenty of time to prepare a recipe. But at school food preparation, eating, and clean up must be done before the class period is over. Either way, you need to plan and manage your time and tasks well.

Working Together

Preparing food in the school lab requires teamwork. The *foods lab* is the kitchen in class. By dividing the tasks, the work goes faster and everyone gets a chance to cook. These qualities are important when you're cooking with others:

- cooperation
- willingness to share
- ability to get along

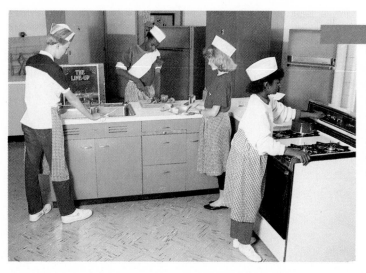

Good results in the foods lab come from cooperation of all individuals. When everyone does their tasks correctly and efficiently the product gets done on time, and it looks and tastes good.

Following a Plan

Preparing food in the school lab usually takes two days. One day is for planning. The other day is for food preparation. When you plan, you might choose a recipe. Remember that time is short at school. Pick recipes that can be prepared within strict time limits. List the foods you'll need. Be sure the school lab has the equipment required.

As part of group planning, divide recipe steps and chores such as dishwashing. Assign tasks so that kitchen work is dovetailed. Rotate the jobs for each lab. Then the same person won't set the table or wash dishes each time. Include clean up time in your planning!

PLANNING TO COOK

Lab_____   Names in Group:
Date_____   _____
Class_____   _____
                                _____
                                _____

Name	Task	Task
Person A	Pick up supplies:	Recipe step #1 Recipe step #5 Wash dishes
Person B	Get out equipment:	Recipe step #2 Recipe step #6 Dry dishes
Person C	Measure ingredients:	Recipe step #3 Recipe step #7 Put dishes away
Person D	Set table:	Recipe step #4 Recipe step #8 Clean table and counters
Evaluation:		

Cleaning Up at School

Cleaning up properly is especially important at school. Many people use the same kitchens. You need to leave the kitchen clean and in order for the next class. Remember that you don't like to work in a kitchen left dirty. Neither do others! Follow these rules for keeping the kitchen clean and neat:

- Keep your work space clean by putting dirty dishes and utensils on a tray while you work. Clean the counter after finishing each task.
- Rinse and stack dishes as you go along. You can wash them faster at a later time if they have already been rinsed. If you have time, wash them as you go.
- Wash all the dishes, utensils, pots, and pans in hot, soapy water.
- Use a dry towel to dry the dishes. There's no time to air dry dishes in the school kitchen.
- Put all the pieces of equipment back in the drawers or cabinets where you found them.

Leave the foods lab neat and clean—as you want to find it at the beginning of your class.

Stacking all the dirty dishes in one place as you work keeps your work area clean and makes the final clean up easier.

Evaluating the Lab

The last step in food preparation is evaluation. To *evaluate* is to judge something. Evaluation is important because you identify what you did right. You also find ways you can do better next time. In the school lab, you might evaluate food preparation with these questions:

- Was our food preparation plan efficient?
- Did everyone in the group cooperate?
- Did the food look good?
- Did the food taste good?
- Was the food served on time?
- Was the kitchen clean when we were done?
- How could we improve?

Cleanliness Around Food

You have already learned to clean up a kitchen. Personal cleanliness around food is important, too. Food must be clean so it's safe to eat. Germs that grow on food cause illnesses, such as colds and flu. *Germs* are tiny living things that you can't see with your eye alone. They spread to food in many ways. One way to keep food clean and safe is to have good habits about personal cleanliness:

- Scrub your hands with soap and water before you prepare food. If you go to the toilet, always wash your hands again before you return to the kitchen. Body wastes are full of germs.
- Wear clean clothes in the kitchen.
- Cover your mouth and nose when you cough or sneeze. Then wash your hands with soap and water right away.
- Keep your hair out of food. Tie long hair back. And don't touch your hair while you cook.
- Wash your hands after you handle raw foods, such as meat or chicken.
- Don't handle food if you have open sores or cuts on your hands. Sores and cuts have germs.

Safety in the Kitchen

Accidents happen. But they don't have to. By being careful and knowing how to work in a safe way, you can avoid many injuries that happen in the kitchen.

- Use dry pot holders when removing foods from the oven.

- Keep paper items and towels away from burners so they don't catch fire.

- Keep handles of pans turned away from the edge of the range to avoid knocking the pan over and burning yourself.

- When removing a lid from a pan of cooking food always hold it at an angle to protect your face from the steam.

- Tie long hair back to avoid catching it on fire when working around a range.

- Put your hands in dishwater gradually to check the temperature. Tap water can be very hot and can burn.

Avoid Burns and Fires

Burns are common kitchen injuries. Stoves and other cooking appliances can cause serious burns or fires if you aren't careful. Remember these rules for avoiding burns and fires:

- Use potholders to handle hot pots and pans. Make sure the potholders are dry, not wet. Heat goes through wet cloth and can cause steam burns. Don't use a dish towel to pick up a hot utensil. It can catch fire if it touches the burner.
- Turn the handles of pots and pans in away from the edge of the stove. You'll be less likely to knock them off. Hot liquids and oils burn if they spill on you.
- Keep long hair away from the burners on the range. Hair catches fire easily. Tie it back. Keep sleeves and loose clothes away from burners, too.
- Keep recipe cards, cookbooks, and towels and potholders away from burners. They also catch fire quickly.
- Checking the soup? Always lift a pot's lid at an angle so it opens away from you. Then the steam won't escape into your face.
- Be careful of burners on a range. They stay hot for a while after they're turned off!
- Water from the faucet can be very hot. Test it, and cool it down if necessary, before you plunge your hands into the dishwater.
- Don't leave the kitchen when you're cooking on a burner. Something could catch fire, and you wouldn't notice. Be especially careful when cooking with oil.
- If a grease fire starts, turn off the burner. Cover the pan with a lid or put baking soda over the fire. Never try to use water to put out a grease fire!

Avoid Cuts

Most cuts come from handling knives in the wrong way. Knives are sharp. Usually they have one sharp edge and one dull edge. To cut, use the sharp side. Learn these rules for knife safety:

- Keep knives sharp. It's easier and less dangerous to cut with a sharp edge than a dull one.
- Be sure your fingers are out of the way when you cut. Cut with the blade going away from your body, then if the knife slips, you won't get cut.

If knives are kept in a drawer they should be kept in a separate section.

- Keep knives in a special place in a drawer or container. Make a cardboard sleeve to put around the blade, or keep knives in a wooden block that has slots to hold the blades.
- Wash knives separately. Don't soak them in the dish water. You might cut yourself if you can't see them in the water.
- When you dry a knife, don't dry with the sharp edge toward your hand.
- Use knives only for cutting food, not for prying lids open.

Two other important rules for avoiding cuts are these. Don't handle broken glass with bare fingers. Sweep it from the floor with a broom. When you open a can, cut the lid off completely and throw it away. Never leave a lid partly attached to a can, and never touch the edge of the lid. It is very sharp.

Keeping cabinet doors closed can prevent bumps on the head.

Avoid Falls and Bumps

A kitchen is a busy place with many opportunities for falls and bumps. Be careful, and be safe.

- Wipe up spills right away.
- Use hot, soapy water to wipe up greasy spills.
- After you wash the floor, let it dry before you walk on it.
- Keep cabinet doors closed so you don't hit your head, poke your eyes, or bump your legs.
- To reach high shelves, stand on a footstool or kitchen ladder. Chairs tip over easily.

Fold and secure any slack in electric cords to prevent pulling them over and burning yourself.

Avoid Electric Shocks

The electricity used to power appliances can give you a shock or even kill you.

- Don't touch an appliance when your hands are wet.
- Keep electric cords out of the way so you don't trip over them or pull appliances over.
- Keep electric cords away from the range.
- Disconnect an appliance if food gets stuck inside. Never remove food from a toaster with a knife.

Planning to Cook

For practice, plan a food lab. Use the chart, "Planning to Cook" on page 110 as your planning sheet. Pretend that you'll prepare the Pineapple-Carrot Salad on page 118. You might make your plan alone or with a group of students. Your teacher will give you directions.

- Copy the planning sheet on a separate piece of paper.
- Write in the names of other students in your group. In many schools, cooking labs have four students each. If your group is a different size, then you'll need to change your lab plan. Your teacher can help you.
- Look at the recipe. What ingredients do you need? Write the names and the amounts of the ingredients on paper.
- Look at the recipe again. Decide what equipment you'll need. The recipe names some utensils, but not all of them.
- Assign food preparation tasks to each person in your group.

This lab plan or a similar one makes food preparation much easier, and it will save you important resources—time and energy!

PINEAPPLE CARROT SALAD

Ingredients

1 8 ¾-ounce can pineapple slices
2 carrots
¼ cup raisins
¼ cup pineapple or orange yogurt
    lettuce leaves
2 tablespoons nuts

Directions

1. Open canned pineapple. With a fork, put pineapple on paper towels to drain. Save juice for another time.
2. Wash carrots. Put on cutting board. Use a sharp knife to cut ends from the carrots. Shred carrots. Put them into a medium bowl.
3. Measure raisins and yogurt. Add to carrots. Stir with a wooden spoon until well mixed.
4. Chop the nuts. Set aside.
5. Wash lettuce and drain on paper towels. For each serving, put one lettuce leaf on a salad plate.
6. Put a pineapple slice on each lettuce leaf.
7. Scoop carrot mixture onto each pineapple slice.
8. Sprinkle chopped nuts on top of salad.
9. Place the salads on the table.

Yield: 4 servings

CHAPTER REVIEW

Summary

After planning a meal and shopping, cooks know that food preparation takes these steps: gathering ingredients and equipment, preparing food, and clean up.

Cooking at school requires special planning and teamwork. A planning sheet is used to assign tasks so that everyone has a chance to cook. Everyone helps with clean up, too.

For safe handling of food, it is important to practice good personal cleanliness habits. This helps stop the spread of germs that cause illness.

Kitchen safety also means avoiding accidents. Burns, cuts, falls and bumps, and electric shocks can be avoided if kitchen equipment is used properly and carefully.

What Have You Learned?

1. What are the steps in preparing food?
2. Name three pre-preparation tasks you might do when following a recipe.
3. What does it mean to dovetail your food preparation tasks?
4. How is cooking at school different from cooking at home?
5. Why should you make a plan for cooking in the school lab?
6. How should a cooking lab be evaluated?
7. Why is cleanliness around food so important?
8. How can you keep food clean and safe to eat?
9. What are three ways to avoid burns in the kitchen? Avoid cuts? Avoid falls and bumps? Avoid electric shocks?

Things to Do

1. Choose a recipe from a cookbook. Write it on paper. List all the pre-preparation steps.
2. Make a list of personal cleanliness rules to post in your lab.
3. Demonstrate one kitchen safety tip to the class.
4. Make kitchen safety posters to hang in the foods laboratory. Each poster should have one rule for avoiding accidents.

START THE DAY WITH BREAKFAST!

balanced breakfast   breakfast which provides about one-fourth of the day's nutrient needs with servings from the main food groups in the Daily Food Guide

breakfast   morning meal

citrus fruit   fruits such as oranges, grapefruits, and tangerines

enriched cereal   refined cereal with vitamins and minerals added

fruit drink   beverage which has only a small amount of real fruit juice

fruit juice   beverage which is 100% real fruit juice with no added water

refined cereal   cereal made from grain after the outer layer of the grain seed or kernel has been removed

whole-grain cereal   cereal made from the entire kernel or seed of grain

CHAPTER 7

After studying this chapter, you should be able to:

- *explain the importance of breakfast.*
- *plan a balanced breakfast with foods from the Daily Food Guide.*
- *compare the nutrients in two breakfast cereals.*
- *prepare a simple breakfast.*

W hat is *breakfast*? "The morning meal," you may say. That's right. The word "breakfast" comes from two words, break and fast. To "fast" means to go without food for a long time. To "break" fast means that you end or interrupt the time of fasting.

From supper at night until the next morning is a long time. When you go without food for so many hours, it's like fasting. People who skip breakfast have a very long fast. You should break your fast with a nutritious morning meal.

Breakfast—A Good Way to Start the Day

Why is a morning meal so important? Your body never stops working. Even as you sleep, your heart beats, you breathe, and your body organs do their work. Food is the fuel which keeps your body going.

In the morning, you need to eat to refuel your body. Then you can be more active, and you will feel your very best. By eating, your body gets the nutrients it needs. Remember that nutrients are protein, carbohydrate, fat, minerals, vitamins, and water.

A good breakfast will help you do better in school. You will be more awake. And perhaps you'll be more interested in your school work. You will probably have more energy for physical activities and sports. You may feel better about everything you do. Eating a good breakfast shows all over.

Some people skip or skimp on breakfast. They think breakfast is fattening. But, a morning meal really helps to control your appetite or the desire to eat. Breakfast eaters don't feel hungry by mid-morning, so they don't want to snack. Did you know that many breakfast skippers or skimpers eat too much at lunchtime?

Breakfasts come in all sizes and the variety of nutritious foods to select from is unlimited.

Overeating Can Be Fattening!

People skip breakfast for many reasons. Some people say they aren't hungry in the morning. But their bodies know they need food. By late morning, they feel hungry. Then they eat more at lunch or nibble on late morning snacks.

What else happens to breakfast skippers? They miss getting many essential nutrients. Many times, they don't make up these missed nutrients up at other meals. They feel tired and have less energy. Their reactions may slow down. They may not think as fast either. People who skip breakfast may get stomach pains and headaches. They may feel grouchy, too.

What Makes a Nutritious Breakfast?

A good breakfast is a balanced breakfast. A *balanced breakfast* provides nutritious foods from the four main food groups in the Daily Food Guide. It should provide about one-fourth of your day's nutrient needs. Since you only need two servings each day from the Meat, Poultry, Fish and Beans Group, you might choose to skip a serving from this group for breakfast. That's fine, but be sure to eat a protein-rich food from the Milk and Cheese Group for breakfast!

A good breakfast has about one-fourth of the calories you need, too. Do you remember what calories are? Calories are the energy value of food. The calories in your meal depend on the foods you eat.

A nutritious breakfast contains foods from each of the food groups.

Use the Food Groups as a Guide

A nutritious breakfast should include:

- one serving from the Milk and Cheese Group. This might be 1 cup of milk, 1 cup of yogurt, or a 1-inch cube of cheese.
- one serving from the Fruit and Vegetable Group. You could have ½ cup of juice or ½ cup of fruit. This is a good time to have a vitamin-C rich fruit. Citrus fruit, melons, mangoes, and strawberries are good examples. *Citrus fruits* include oranges, grapefruit, and tangerines. Many breakfast skippers don't get enough vitamin C. Remember that vitamin C is an important nutrient. It helps your body fight infections and disease. It also helps maintain healthy gums.
- one serving from the Bread and Cereal Group. You might choose a slice of toast, a bowl of cereal, or a tortilla from this group.
- one serving from the Meat, Poultry, Fish, and Beans Group. A serving from this food group could be 2 eggs, or 2 to 3 ounces cooked, lean meat or poultry. You only need two servings from this group each day. You might prefer a smaller portion from this group in the morning. Then you can eat a larger serving at your noon or evening meal. A food from the Fats and Sweets Group adds extra flavor. Butter or jam on bread are two examples. Eat these foods in small amounts. They provide calories but few nutrients.

Creating a Breakfast Menu

Your breakfast menu should be balanced. A balanced menu has a variety of foods from the four main food groups. The choices depend on your likes and needs. Each person is a little different. For example, what do you like to eat? How hungry are you? Are you physically active? How much time do you have for breakfast? Your answers to these questions are important. They will help you plan a breakfast that will be right for you.

The more active you are, the more calories your body needs. Breakfast should supply about one-fourth of them.

A Big or Small Breakfast?

Some people like a big meal in the morning. If they do heavy physical work, they need more calories. Growing teenagers often have big appetites. They may need more nutrients and calories than most adults do. A big breakfast might include:

Fruit or Fruit Juice
Breakfast Cereal
Eggs and/or Meat
Bread
Milk

People who are less active need fewer calories. But they still need to eat a balanced diet. People who want to lose weight might want a light meal. This is one menu for a light breakfast:

Fruit or Fruit Juice
Breakfast Cereal or Bread
Milk

People with average appetites might add eggs or cheese to a light breakfast. Do you prefer a small meal or a big meal in the morning? Why? You can certainly choose a breakfast that matches your likes and needs.

LOW-CALORIE BREAKFAST MENUS

The calories in breakfast depend on what you choose. If you want a low-calorie menu, try these menus:

- For 235 calories eat ½ cup grapefruit juice, 1 cup plain cornflakes, 1 cup skim milk.
- For 270 calories eat 1 orange, 1 small waffle, 1 cup skim milk, 1 teaspoon butter or margarine.
- For 300 calories eat 1 scrambled egg, 1 slice toast, 1 teaspoon butter or margarine, ¼ cantaloupe, 1 cup skim milk.

BREAKFAST FOODS CAN BE ANY NUTRITIOUS FOODS

Use these ideas as part of a balanced breakfast:

- Melon half filled with yogurt and granola
- Breakfast shake made with milk, fruit, and ice cream
- Bagel with cream cheese, strawberries, and milk
- Whole-grain crackers, cheese, and fruit
- Peanut butter and banana sandwich, milk
- Cold, fried chicken with carrot and cheese sticks

Something Different for Breakfast

Some people don't like usual breakfast foods. Others are tired of eating the same breakfast foods. Why not try something different?

Breakfast foods can be any foods you like. You can eat foods like cereal with milk, toast, and juice. Or you can enjoy a peanut butter sandwich with milk. Your body only knows that you are eating nutrients. The nutrients in any balanced meal will help you break the fast. What other interesting breakfast foods can you think of?

Even common breakfasts can have special interest. You might sprinkle a waffle with sliced fruit. Or you could spread apple butter on whole-wheat toast.

While these breakfasts might seem unusual to you they are certainly nutritious. And they're quick to fix.

Quick-to-Fix Breakfasts

You don't have to skip breakfast, even if you sleep late. Make a quick breakfast. Plan ahead so you make time to eat. You might get everything ready the night before. Prepare quick-to-fix foods.

If time is really short, find foods you can eat on your way to school. Crackers, cheese, and an apple would get your day off to a nutritious start. But it isn't a good idea to eat on the run all the time. It's hard to eat a variety of nutritious foods when you eat this way.

Breakfast Ideas for People Who Aren't Hungry

Some people aren't hungry when they wake up. Do you fall into this group? Then delay your meal a bit. Get dressed first. Take out the dog. Straighten your room or review your homework. Then eat breakfast.

Start with a light meal. Then add something more each day. Start with some juice or fruit. Later add crackers or bread. Then balance the meal with milk, cheese, peanut butter, an egg, or meat. These simple ideas may help you become a breakfast eater in no time.

If you're not hungry when you first get up, delay breakfast until you've gotten dressed and walked the dog or straightened your room.

Cereals—A Good Morning Food

Cereals are common breakfast foods. In cold weather, many people like hot cereals, such as grits or oatmeal. Dry cereals such as cornflakes, raisin bran, or puffed rice are popular throughout the year. Other breakfast foods are made from grains, too. Bread, waffles, tortillas, and bagels are some examples.

Breakfast Cereals Are Grain Products

Cereals are made from grains. Food manufacturers turn grains into food people can eat. Before some grains are made into cereals to serve on the table, they are *refined*. This means the outer coat, or layer, of the grain kernel is removed. The outer layer of the grain has many nutrients. When this layer is not used in refined cereals, nutrients are lost.

To make refined cereals more healthful, manufacturers replace the minerals and vitamins which were lost. These improved cereals are called *enriched*.

When the outer layer or shell of the grain is left in the cereal, it is called *whole-grain cereal*. It is made from the whole kernel of grain. Whole-grain cereal has more natural nutrients and fiber than enriched cereals. The outer layer isn't thrown away. The most nutritious grain products are enriched or whole-grain. When you shop, look for those words on the label.

Some breakfast cereals are presweetened. This means they have sugar added. Granola is one example. Sugar-coated cornflakes are another example. Many Americans eat too much sugar. One way to cut back is to choose cereals without sugar. You can add fruit instead of sugar if you want a sweeter taste. Fruit gives you nutrients along with the sweet flavor.

The most common cereals are made from wheat, corn, rice, and oats. Can you name any others?

Whole-grain and enriched cereals are good sources of carbohydrates, iron, and B vitamins. The carbohydrate in grain products provides energy. Whole-grains are also a good source of fiber.

Flour is made from grains. Flour is used to make bread, waffles, muffins, and many other foods you enjoy at breakfast time. Most flour is enriched.

A cereal package gives you a lot of information. The ingredient list gives the ingredients in order. It begins with the ingredients present in the largest amount and goes down to those present in the least amount. If sugar or honey are in the first two or three ingredients, the cereal probably has been presweetened.

Many foods common to all of us are made from cereal grains.

1 Measure cereal and water carefully, according to directions.

4 Stir cereal and water until they are completely blended. This keeps the cereal from getting lumpy.

2 Bring water to a boil in a covered saucepan.

5 Cook at a low temperature, according to package directions. Most hot cereals cook from 5 to 10 minutes. Precooked or instant cereals usually take 2 to 3 minutes.

3 Slowly pour dry cereal into boiling water with one hand. With your other hand, use a spoon to stir the cereal constantly.

6 Serve hot.

Preparing Breakfast Cereals

Dry cereal is easy to serve. You just need to put it in a bowl and pour on milk. For extra nutrients, flavor, and variety, add sliced fruit or chopped nuts. Cooked cereals take a little longer to prepare, but you can make them easily. Just follow the package instructions. Cooked cereals taste good with a sprinkling of cinnamon or chopped nuts.

Serving cold or hot cereals is a matter of personal taste and sometimes, the weather. Hot cereal is often more enjoyable in cold weather. Cold cereals are good any time.

The nutrients in cold and hot cereals are about the same. Read the package labels to see just which nutrients a cereal contains. When you add milk or fruit to cereal, you also add nutrients.

Beverages with a Morning Meal

Most breakfast menus include at least one beverage. Beverages are the best source of water—an important nutrient. Besides satisfying thirst, most beverages provide many nutrients, too. The ingredients in beverages determine the nutrient value. Nutritious beverages are described below.

Beverages Made with Milk

Milk and hot chocolate made from milk are excellent sources of calcium. Calcium helps you build strong bones and teeth.

You can choose from several types of milk. Whole milk, low-fat milk, and skim milk all have a similar amount of nutrients. But they have different amounts of fat. Whole milk has the most fat. It also has the most calories. Skim milk has the fewest calories and least fat. Low-fat milk has less calories and fat than whole milk, but more than skim milk. Choose the one that's best for you.

By blending cocoa mix with cold or hot milk, you can make chocolate milk or hot chocolate. These beverages are nutritious, too. You get the nutrients from milk with a few extra calories from the cocoa mix. Many good blender breakfasts are made from milk and fruit. All the ingredients are mixed in a blender.

There are several types of milk. Whole milk has the most fat and therefore the most calories. Skim milk has the least. Low-fat milk is in between.

Fruit Beverages

Many juices are delicious for breakfast. Orange, grapefruit, and apple juice are good choices. You can buy juice in many forms. It comes canned, refrigerated, and frozen as a concentrate. A fruit concentrate has much of the water removed by the manufacturer. You mix in water before you serve it. Just follow directions on the package. You can also squeeze your own fresh orange or grapefruit juice. These juices are good sources of vitamin C.

Sometimes people confuse fruit juices and fruit drinks. *Fruit juice* is 100% real fruit juice with no water added. *Fruit drinks* are not as nutritious. They are made with only a small amount of real fruit juice. The rest is sugar, water, and added vitamin C. The label on the beverage container identifies a fruit beverage as a juice or a drink.

You get more nutrients per serving from juice.

Make Breakfast Easily!

Here is a simple breakfast that you can prepare quickly. It is also a nutritious meal.

MENU 1

Breakfast

Juice
French Toast
Milk

Preparing the Breakfast

1. Take the fruit juice and milk from the refrigerator. If you have frozen juice concentrate, you will have to mix it with water. Get a pitcher large enough to hold the juice. Open the can of concentrate and pour it into the pitcher. The can tells how much water to add to the concentrate. Stir until the water and concentrate are well blended.
2. Prepare French Toast. You can find a recipe in most cookbooks. Follow the directions carefully.
3. Serve the French Toast on a plate, with syrup or fruit.
4. Pour milk and juice into the glasses. By filling glasses and bowls on the counter, you keep your table clean.
5. Place the food on the table.

Clean Up Time

When the meal is over, it's time to clean up.

1. Remove the dishes from the table.
2. Rinse, stack, and wash the dishes.
3. After the dishes have been dried, put them back where they belong.

Starting Breakfast the Night Before

Do you like to get few extra winks of sleep in the morning? You can sleep a little longer, and still eat a relaxed and nutritious breakfast. The trick is to do some steps ahead.

- Keep ingredients on hand. Then you will have choices available to you.
- Have your equipment ready. Get bowls and spoons out.
- Have the frying pan ready if you need it.
- Prepare some foods ahead. You can start getting some foods ready the night before. This will save time in the morning.

  Juice. Mix frozen juice with water. Cover and refrigerate. Canned juices don't need mixing. Chill canned juice in the refrigerator.

  Cold cereal. Pour the cereal into a bowl. Cover the bowl with foil or plastic wrap.

  Waffles or pancakes. You can buy frozen waffles or ready-to-pour pancake batter. These save time. They may also cost more than making your own. You can mix your own pancake or waffle batter the night before, then cover and refrigerate it. You can also freeze leftover waffles. First let them cool, then place them in a plastic bag or freezer container. Put them in the freezer. For a quick breakfast, heat up a frozen waffle in the toaster.

  Another trick helps get you ready for breakfast. Go to sleep a few minutes earlier. Then you can wake up earlier, too. You will have the time to start your day with nutritious food. It is worth the effort to "break" your "fast!"

Heating frozen waffles in the toaster is fast. Next time you make waffles freeze the left overs for another time.

CHAPTER REVIEW

Summary

Breakfast gives you the nutrients you need to begin the day. A good breakfast follows the food group guidelines. Morning is a good time to eat a vitamin C-rich fruit. Any nutritious food can make a good breakfast food.

Breakfast cereals are made from grains. Most nutritious cereals are enriched or whole-grain. Package labels tell you which nutrients and ingredients are in the cereal. Beverages such as milk and fruit juice at breakfast provide water and other important nutrients.

Breakfast can be made quickly when everything is gathered before starting to cook, and when some things are prepared the night before.

What Have You Learned?

1. Why do you need a good breakfast?
2. Name some foods that are high in vitamin C.
3. List three quick-to-fix, nutritious breakfast ideas.
4. Define enriched, refined, and whole-grain.
5. How can you tell which nutrients and ingredients are found in cereals?
6. What nutritious beverages might you serve for breakfast?
7. How can you make breakfast an easy meal to prepare?

Things to Do

1. Create a breakfast poster telling why breakfast is important.
2. Bring to class an empty cereal box. What grain is it made from? Find the words "enriched" or "whole-grain." Write what they mean. What minerals and vitamins are found in the cereal? Explain what five of these nutrients do.
3. Bring an empty container from a fruit juice or drink to class. Read the label. Write down the ingredients in the product. What does this information tell you?

BRUNCH IS A SPECIAL MEAL

bake	to cook in the oven using dry heat
brunch	meal served in late morning, which usually serves as both breakfast and lunch
convenience foods	foods that save you time because they are partly prepared when you buy them
flatware	knives, forks, and spoons
frying	cooking in fat or oil
hard-cooked eggs	eggs which are simmered until the yolks and whites are firm
place setting	arrangement of dishes, glassware, flatware, and napkin for one person at a meal
preheat	to heat the oven to the temperature you need before using it for cooking
scrambled eggs	eggs which are stirred, then cooked in fat
simmer	cook in water just below the boiling point

After reading this chapter, you should be able to:

- *plan, prepare, and serve a nutritious brunch.*
- *describe how to cook bacon and sausage.*
- *explain how to make muffins from a mix.*

S undays and holidays are special days! Older family members might not work on those days, and you don't go to school. Perhaps you all sleep a little later.

When you have more time in the morning, it's fun to have a hearty and special breakfast, or a *brunch*. This word is made from two words, "breakfast" and "lunch." It's one meal to take the place of two! Usually, brunch is served late in the morning. Brunch can offer variety to the week's breakfasts. Serving brunch is also a nice way to entertain guests.

137

Brunch Foods

What foods are good for brunch? Serve any nutritious foods you enjoy for breakfast or lunch. Since brunch takes the place of two meals, make it a bigger meal. Like other meals, a good brunch has a balanced menu. Remember that a balanced meal has foods from the four main food groups.

Usually, brunch is relaxing because you have plenty of time to prepare it and to enjoy eating it. With more time, you also have more menu choices. For example, you might take the time to prepare eggs and bacon.

Convenience foods are also good for brunch. A *convenience food* is partly prepared when you buy it so it saves food-preparation time. Ready-to-bake biscuits and muffin mixes are both convenience foods. What others can you think of?

Many restaurants serve brunch on the weekends—often buffet style. Notice the combination of traditional breakfast foods along with other foods.

Eggs—A Good Brunch Food

Eggs are a good brunch food and can be served in many different ways. Recipes with eggs as the main ingredient are good for any meal and for snacks. Remember that an ingredient is one item in a recipe.

Eggs are a valuable source of protein and iron. Protein builds and repairs your body. Iron is an important part of your blood. Both protein and iron are nutrients.

Wise shoppers know that eggs have a lot of protein, yet they do not cost a lot. Eggs are bought by size and each size has a different weight. Bigger eggs cost more, but you also get more. The next time you shop for groceries, notice the sizes and prices of eggs. After you buy eggs take them home and refrigerate them until you are ready to use them. Don't wash them. This takes away the protective coating.

EGG SUBSTITUTES

Eggs are an important source of nutrients in the diet. Egg yolks are also high in cholesterol. Scientists do not yet know for certain, but there is evidence that too much cholesterol in the diet may increase the risk of heart disease.

Egg substitutes have been developed for people who are on low-cholesterol or low-calorie diets. They have less cholesterol and saturated fat than eggs, and they are lower in calories. However, they also have less protein and phosphorus than eggs. Some egg substitutes do not have all the B vitamins found in eggs.

Most egg substitutes are made by combining egg whites with ingredients that take the place of the yolk. The substitutes are available in liquid, frozen, and dried forms. They can be used for scrambled eggs, omelets, and in recipes.

Cooking Eggs   There is one simple rule for cooking eggs. Keep the temperature low. If you cook eggs at a high temperature, they get tough.

Eggs are used as the main ingredient in many recipes. For brunch, you might serve fried, scrambled, or hard-cooked eggs.

Frying means to cook in fat or oil. To fry eggs, remove them from their shell and cook them in a frying pan with a little hot fat. Margarine or butter works fine, but be sure the fat isn't too hot. You can check it by adding a drop of water to the hot fat. If it sizzles, it's ready. When the fat is too hot, the edges of the egg will turn brown and curl. Very hot fat can also catch fire.

To *scramble* eggs, stir the whites and yolks together with a fork. Then pour the mixture into a little hot fat in a frying pan and continue to stir. Scrambled eggs cook fast. When the pan is too hot, they cook too fast and become very dry or burn. You should cook them slowly over low heat.

Some people like *hard-cooked* eggs for brunch. They are made by simmering eggs in their shell for 15–20 minutes. The yolks and whites get hard. Soft-cooked eggs have soft yolks. They simmer for only 4–6 minutes. To *simmer* is to cook in water just below the boiling point. Water is simmering when bubbles appear only along the edge of the pan, not in the middle like boiling water.

Eggs are an important ingredient in a lot of recipes. They're also served alone in a variety of ways. They're often served at brunches.

Hard-cooked eggs that are boiled too long develop a green ring around the yolk. The whites also turn rubbery and tough.

Add Flavor with Bacon or Sausage

Think of the mouth-watering smell of bacon or sausage in the morning. They taste so good with eggs, pancakes, and waffles. Like eggs, breakfast meats provide protein. Breakfast meats may also be high in fat. Both protein and fat have calories to give you energy. Remember that calories are the energy value of food.

Keep bacon and sausage fresh and safe to eat until you cook them. Cover them tightly in a plastic container or a plastic bag. Store them in the refrigerator and use them within two weeks. You can freeze them both so they will keep longer.

Bacon or sausage is often fried. Because these meats have so much fat, you don't need to add extra fat. You just cook them in a frying pan over medium heat.

Bacon cooks faster than sausage. When bacon is done, the strips shrivel and get smaller. The color changes and becomes slightly golden as the strips stiffen. Be careful, however, as bacon will dry out or burn if it cooks too long, or if the cooking temperature is too high. Sausage browns nicely when it's cooked on all sides. It should be well done but not dried out.

Baked Quick Breads—Hot from the Oven

Bread is often part of a brunch menu. Bread is usually baked in the oven. Can you define the term *bake*? It means to cook in an oven with dry heat.

Some breads are quick to make. They are called quick breads. That's because the batter is prepared, then immediately popped in the oven. Batter is a thin mixture of flour, liquid, and other ingredients.

There is a wide variety of quick breads available. You can make them from scratch or you can use convenience foods like you see here.

Quick breads are light and airy because the batter fills with air bubbles as it cooks. In quick breads, baking powder and baking soda are used as ingredients to make air bubbles very fast causing the bread batter to rise quickly as it cooks. Muffins, waffles, biscuits, coffee cakes, and pancakes are examples of quick breads.

Some quick breads are packaged as convenience foods. Muffin mixes are an example. You can also make quick breads from scratch.

For brunch, you might prepare muffins from a mix, or make biscuits from refrigerated dough. Dough is a thick mixture of flour and other ingredients. It is thicker than batter. To make muffins or biscuits, read the instructions on the package. Get out the equipment and ingredients. Then carefully follow the directions.

When making quick breads from scratch, mixing is an important step. Mix only to blend the ingredients. Don't mix too much or you will get big holes in the muffins or bread. This will make your quick breads small and heavy.

For variety, mix chopped nuts or fruit into the batter before you bake it. Or make surprise muffins by putting a small amount of batter into the muffin pan, adding a teaspoon of jelly or jam, and then covering this with more batter.

Let's Make Brunch

Here's a nutritious brunch menu that you might prepare in class. It's also perfect to make at home for your family. The amount you prepare depends on how many people you serve.

Look at the menu. Can you put each food into a food group? Remember that a balanced meal has foods from each of the four main food groups.

MENU 1	
Easy Family Brunch	**Baked Apple Slices** **Bacon and Eggs** **Hot Muffins Jam and Butter** **Milk**

How much should you make? Prepare one egg, two bacon strips, one apple, and at least one muffin per person.

When making any quick bread from a mix be sure to follow the directions carefully.

Baking Muffins

1. Choose any convenience muffin mix.
2. Read the package directions.
3. Preheat the oven according to directions. *Preheat* means to let the oven get to the temperature you need before using it to bake.
4. Grease the muffin pans so the muffins won't stick to the pans.
5. Gather equipment and measure ingredients.
6. Follow directions to prepare the batter. Stir the batter with a fork just until the ingredients are blended.
7. Fill muffin pans about two-thirds full.
8. Bake according to the package directions. Cool in the pan at least five minutes before serving.

Making Baked Apple Slices

1. Wash the apples. Cut each into four equal parts. Remove the stems and cores, and throw them away. Put the apple slices into individual baking dishes.
2. Sprinkle one teaspoon lemon juice and one-fourth teaspoon cinnamon on top of each apple.
3. Top with a little granola or brown sugar.
4. Bake until soft, 15 minutes or more. You can bake them in the oven with the muffins at 400° F. The apples will be soft when the muffins are done, but they'll still keep their shape.
5. While the apples are baking, pour milk into a pitcher. Keep the pitcher of milk in the refrigerator until you are ready to serve. Serve the milk with the baked apple slices.
6. Keep the baked apple slices warm until ready to serve. Serve in the individual baking dishes.

After bacon is cooked it needs to be drained on paper towels to remove excess grease.

Frying Bacon

1. Separate the strips of bacon. Place them in a large, cold frying pan.
2. Cook over a medium heat until the strips are crisp and golden brown. This takes about five to seven minutes. Turn with a fork or tongs as the bacon browns.
3. When the bacon is done, it is stiff and golden brown. Turn the heat off and remove the bacon strips from the hot fat with a fork or tongs. Drain the strips on paper towels and blot the grease with another paper towel if needed.
4. Save the bacon fat for the eggs.
5. Cover the bacon to keep it warm until you are ready to serve it.

Cooking Fried Eggs

1. Spoon off some of the bacon fat left in the frying pan from frying the bacon. Leave one or two tablespoons of fat in the pan for frying eggs. Or use margarine or butter.
2. Turn the heat to a medium temperature. Have the fat just hot enough so a drop of water sizzles in it.
3. Crack one egg carefully into a cup. Try to keep the egg yolk whole.
4. Gently slide the egg out of the cup into the hot fat.
5. Repeat until you have all the eggs in the pan. Use a frying pan that's the right size. Most frying pans hold two or four eggs. If you cook more eggs, make two batches.
6. Cover the pan. Cook for two or three minutes until the eggs are firm around the edges.
7. Turn off heat and remove eggs one at a time from the pan with a turner. Put the eggs on a warm plate and put the bacon around the eggs.

Setting the Brunch Table

Setting the table nicely for brunch can add to its enjoyment. You might do this while you are waiting for the muffins to bake. Colorful placemats or tablecloths make a meal seem more special. If you're using a table covering, put it on the table first.

Now, what dishes will you need for serving brunch? The apples may be served in the bowls in which they were cooked. Large dinner plates are best for the bacon and eggs.

What pieces of flatware will you need? *Flatware* includes knives, forks, and spoons. You will need all of these for this menu.

Look at the table setting diagram to see how the flatware, plate, glass, and napkin are placed for each place setting. A *place setting* includes the dishes, glass, flatware, and napkin for one person at a table.

Colorful place mats and a centerpiece can make a meal more enjoyable.

Careful timing is important if you're going to serve hot foods hot and cold foods cold.

Timing the Meal

To make the brunch really good, serve all the hot foods hot. That's why you kept the bacon in a warm place. And serve the cold foods, such as milk, cold.

Timing is most important for any meal you serve. You want the foods ready at the same time so everything will be at the right temperature. To plan your time, find out how long each food needs to cook. First, cook the food that takes the longest. For this meal, the muffins and the baked apple slices will take the longest time. They should be made first.

Cook the bacon before the eggs. They can be cooked in the same pan. Start the bacon about ten minutes after the muffins have gone into the oven.

Hints for Serving

- Place butter and jam on the table for the muffins.
- Pour the milk into the glasses.
- Serve the baked apple slices in the small bowls. Do you have milk in a pitcher to serve with them?
- Serve the bacon, eggs, and muffins. Remember to have a serving spoon and fork ready. Cover the muffins with a napkin to keep them warm.

Covering biscuits or muffins with a napkin will help to keep them warm.

Everyone should participate in conversation at the table. Try to avoid unpleasant topics so that the meal is an enjoyable one.

- You may serve the bacon and eggs in one of several ways. Serving platters filled with food may be passed around the table. Or the food may be placed on the individual plates in the kitchen and served. Individual plates are served from the kitchen so the place settings are set without the dinner plate.

Pleasant conversation is part of an enjoyable meal. Whether you have guests or just your famiy, you should take part in the conversation. What interesting things could you talk about?

Proper Clean-Up Is Part of the Meal

Did you clean up carefully? Did you wash the dishes carefully? Were all dishes returned to the right places? Did you put the tablecloth or placemats away carefully? Did you brush up crumbs and wipe the stove and countertops? Were the kitchen and eating areas left neat?

Evaluating Brunch

To evaluate means to judge and plan for improvement. Evaluate your brunch by answering these questions. Did you enjoy your meal? Was the food good? Did you like eating with your classmates? Now, list everything that made this a good meal.

Did anything go wrong? Write it down. How could you do better next time? Make a list of these ideas.

You have now made two lists. You have evaluated your brunch. This means that you thought about the good points and the bad points. Then you decided whether the meal was good or bad. When you evaluate a meal, you will probably remember how to make the next meal even better.

Evaluating your group's performance after each lab will help you improve.

CHAPTER REVIEW

Summary

Brunch is breakfast and lunch combined. Almost any nutritious food can be served for brunch. Eggs can be cooked in many ways—scrambled, fried, and hard-cooked. Bacon and sausage are usually fried. Quick breads can be made from scratch, or you may use convenience foods.

Meals like brunch should be carefully planned so that they are enjoyable. Foods should be prepared so they can be served at the right temperatures. A carefully set table can add to the enjoyment of a meal. Good conversation makes a meal pleasant. The meal should be evaluated so it can be improved, if necessary, the next time.

What Have You Learned?

1. List five foods that could be served for brunch.
2. What happens if you cook eggs at a temperature which is too high?
3. How do you make scrambled eggs? Fried eggs? Hard-cooked eggs?
4. How do you cook bacon? Sausage?
5. What happens if you mix quick bread batter too much?
6. Describe a convenience food.
7. How do you make muffins from a mix?
8. What can you do to make sure hot foods are served hot?
9. How might you arrange a place setting for brunch?
10. What points should you think about when you evaluate a meal?

Things to Do

1. Plan three menus for brunch: for your family, for three school friends as guests, for your family and two relatives. Discuss your menus with the class. Tell why you chose a different menu for different people.
2. Discuss the different ways you could serve bacon and eggs at the table. Which way seems best to you? Why?
3. Take a trip to the grocery store. Find five different breads that are convenience foods. Describe them.

PACK AND GO MEALS

chemical cold pack	something which helps keep food cold and is colder than ice
insulated container	container which protects food from cold or heat for a short time
peel	to remove the skin from food
sandwich	two or more slices of bread with food placed between them
sandwich spread	food spread on bread to keep it moist
spoiled food	food which is no longer safe to eat
wax paper	paper with a coating of wax to protect it from moisture

After reading this chapter, you should be able to:

- *plan a nutritious packed lunch.*
- *demonstrate how to make and wrap a sandwich.*
- *describe how to prepare fresh fruit and vegetables for a carried meal.*
- *explain how to make refrigerated cookies.*
- *prepare an appealing packed meal.*
- *describe five ways to keep carried food safe.*

D o you get excited when you receive a gift-wrapped package? If you're like most people, you admire the wrapping. Maybe you shake it and examine the shape. You want to know what's inside.

A meal you pack for school or an outing can also be attractive and interesting. Peek inside a lunch bag or picnic basket and hopefully you'll find a healthful meal that looks good and tastes terrific! Healthful foods are both nutritious and safe to eat.

A Meal to Carry With You

Whether it's breakfast, lunch, or supper, a packed meal should be nutritionally balanced. A balanced diet has foods from all four main food groups. These carefully chosen foods give you energy for work and fun. Balanced meals also provide the variety of nutrients your body needs to do its work.

A healthful meal stays fresh and safe because the foods don't spoil quickly. Eating *spoiled food* could make you sick.

A pack-and-go meal should look good several hours after you make it, even if it's been tossed in a locker or squeezed into a school bag.

Foods that are good to carry:

- won't spoil quickly out of the refrigerator.
- don't crush easily.
- won't get soggy.
- can be eaten with your fingers.
- can be carried easily.

A peanut butter sandwich packs well. Can you name other foods that pack well?

Many factory workers carry their lunch to work everyday just as many students carry a lunch to school. Why are some of these lunches better than others?

Sandwiches—A Good Lunch Bag Food

A sandwich is a popular food for a carried meal. Why? You're right if you said that sandwiches are easy to make, carry, and eat.

Most *sandwiches* have two or more slices of bread with food placed between them. A good sandwich has:

- bread that isn't dry or soggy
- butter or margarine to keep the bread moist
- a filling, spread to the corners of the bread, or slices of meat or cheese
- ingredients for extra flavor, such as lettuce or pickles

You can make sandwich-eating interesting. Just change the type of bread and the fillings to make a different sandwich for each day of the week.

A typical sandwich gives you two servings from the Bread and Cereal Group. What kind of bread do you like for sandwiches? Enriched white bread and whole-wheat bread are the most common. Earlier you learned about enriched and whole-grain products. Whole-wheat bread is made from whole-grain flour.

The supermarket shelf has other delicious breads, too. For example, try sandwiches on rye bread or raisin bread. Rolls and pocket bread make good sandwiches, too. Next time you go food shopping, notice the variety of sandwich breads.

Sandwich fillings can be very nutritious. They usually include foods from the Meat, Poultry, Fish, and Beans Group. What good fillings have you had in a sandwich? Ham, chicken, and bologna are good examples. Sliced cheese from the Milk and Cheese Group tastes good, too. Remember that cheese is a good source of calcium. Calcium helps build strong bones and teeth.

A *sandwich spread* keeps bread moist. You might like butter or margarine as the sandwich spread. For extra flavor, try mustard instead. Many people especially like mustard on ham sandwiches. Crisp lettuce leaves, tomato slices, and pickles are good. What else could you add?

BREAD TALK

White bread, made from white flour, is the most common bread in this country. Another kind of bread that people are baking and is being seen more and more at supermarkets is whole wheat bread. Both of these breads contain important nutrients. But whole wheat bread has more fiber and contains more trace minerals than white bread. So it's a good idea to include some whole wheat bread in your diet.

Whole wheat bread is light brown in color. That's because the flour the bread is made from uses the whole grain of wheat—including the parts that make flour dark, the bran and the wheat germ. But, be careful, just because bread is brown doesn't mean it's whole wheat bread.

Sometimes bread manufacturers add coloring to white bread to make it look brown. It may be brown, but it's not any more nutritious. If you want a whole grain bread, check the ingredient label to see that all the flour in the bread is *whole* grain flour. If the ingredients list things like "flour," "wheat flour" or even "unbleached enriched wheat flour," that is all white flour, and it's not a whole grain bread.

Raw Vegetables—Good Finger Foods

Raw vegetables are great for a packed lunch because they carry well and are good finger foods.

Vegetables are important in a balanced diet. Remember that you need four servings from the Fruit and Vegetable Group each day. Some raw vegetables, such as carrots and green peppers, are high in vitamin A. Vitamin A helps you see better at night in the dark. Vegetables also have fiber, which helps the body get rid of its waste. Earlier, you learned that people control their body weight by controlling the number of calories they eat. Raw vegetables are good foods for weight-watchers because they are low in calories.

What raw vegetables might you pack and eat later? Carrot and celery sticks taste great as do cucumber slices, green pepper sticks, or even raw broccoli. Many people enjoy raw vegetables as snacks or as part of a meal.

Raw vegetables, washed and cut into bite sized pieces are tasty and nutritious foods for a packed lunch.

Fresh Fruit

Fruit can be a welcome addition to a packed meal. Fresh fruit such as an apple or banana, is easiest to carry. Or pack a peach, some grapes, or cherries for variety. Late summer and early fall will provide you with many choices of fresh fruit.

Many fruits are good sources of vitamin C. Remember that vitamin C helps protect you from illness. Like vegetables, some fruits are also good sources of vitamin A and fiber.

The outer skin of fruit has the most fiber so you should eat apples, pears, and peaches with their skins on. Be sure to wash the fruit first. Washing removes any chemical that may have been sprayed on the fruit as well as any dirt. Wash the fruit in clean, cold water as you gently rub the surface.

The skins of some fruits can't be eaten. You need to *peel* both bananas and oranges by pulling their skin off. An orange peel is sometimes harder to remove. When you make a packed lunch in class, you'll learn how to peel an orange easily.

Cookies, Cookies, and More

Cookies are easy to make and often a welcome lunch bag dessert. Firm cookies don't get easily crushed in a lunch bag.

There are many different kinds of cookies. Cookies are made from a thick mixture of flour, liquid, and other ingredients, called dough.

Drop cookies are made by dropping dough from a spoon onto a cookie sheet and then baking them. Remember that baking is cooking in the oven using dry heat.

Rolled cookies are so named because first you roll the dough. Then you cut it into fancy shapes and place it on a cookie sheet to bake.

Brownies are bar cookies. You pour the brownie batter into a pan and bake. They you cut them into squares.

Refrigerator cookies are made in two steps. First, you make the dough and roll it into a log. Then you wrap it carefully in wax paper or aluminum foil. *Wax paper* has a coating of wax to protect it from moisture. The dough is refrigerated until it gets stiff, which takes several hours or overnight. The second step is to slice the cookies onto a cookie sheet. Then you bake them. You can buy refrigerator dough in the grocery store. Then you just slice and bake!

Cookies generally belong in the Fats and Sweets Group. They have a lot of sugar and fat, but few nutrients. Butter and margarine in cookie dough are both fats. Cookies mainly contribute calories to your diet, but you can make cookies more nutritious by adding nuts or raisins to the dough. Oatmeal and pumpkin cookies are more nutritious than sugar or butter cookies.

Drop cookies.
Rolled cookies.
Bar cookies.
Refrigerator cookies.

FOODS FOR THE PACKED LUNCH

Sandwiches or Hearty Food	Fruit	Vegetables	Other Food
fried chicken	apple	carrot sticks	peanuts
hard-cooked eggs	banana	celery sticks	sunflower seeds
ham sandwich on rye bread	grapes or nectarine	green pepper circles	fruit juice or pickles
peanut butter on enriched white bread	peach or pear	broccoli pieces	oatmeal cookies
cream cheese on raisin bread	plums or raisins	cauliflower pieces	whole-wheat muffin
crackers and cheese bologna and cheese on enriched white bread	dried apples	cucumber slices	soup (in thermos)
What might you add to the list?			

Other Good Foods to Carry

What else might you pack to eat? Raisins and other dried fruits are substitutes for fresh fruit. Cheese cubes won't spoil at room temperature. Pickles add flavor. Peanuts are crunchy foods that are a good source of protein. Canned juice is a good drink. For lunch at school, remember to bring milk money!

Packing a Carried Meal

Your meal needs to be carefully packed. A good packing job keeps food looking and tasting good. It also stays fresh longer.

Wrapping Sandwiches

After you make a sandwich, wrap it so it stays moist and doesn't get dry. You can store sandwiches in plastic bags or use plastic containers with tight-fitting lids. Wax paper, plastic wrap, or aluminum foil will also do a good job. Look at the photos on the next page. Then follow the directions for wrapping a sandwich.

HOW TO WRAP A SANDWICH

1 Cut your sandwich in pieces that are easy to handle.

2 Place the sandwich in the center of a piece of wax paper. The paper should be big enough so that it will cover the sandwich and overlap at the edges.

3 Hold the two edges of the long side together and fold the edges twice so the fold lies flat on the sandwich.

4 Fold the end edges toward the center to form a point. Tuck the two points under the sandwich.

Packing the Lunch Bag or Box

A lunch bag is a good container for carrying food because you can throw it away after the meal.

Most lunch boxes are made of metal or heavy plastic to protect food from crushing. Caution: You must keep the lunch box clean. Wash it with hot, soapy water every time it's used. Rinse with very hot water and dry carefully. Leave it open to the air when you're not using it.

When you pack a lunch:

- Wrap each food separately.
- Put the heaviest foods on the bottom.
- Put lighter things on top.
- Tuck small things in corners.
- Include a napkin.
- Put in a spoon or any other utensil you will need.
- Don't put in foods that spoil quickly.

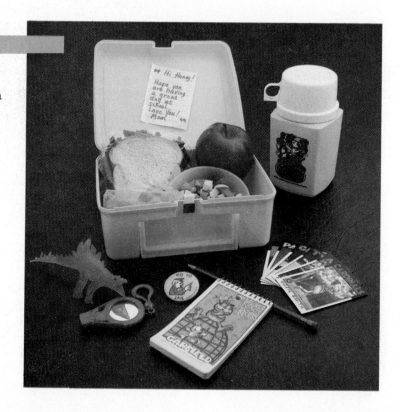

You can make a child's lunch special by adding a surprise once in a while.

Surprises Make Lunch Special!

Remember the special gift package we talked about in the beginning of the chapter? Something very interesting was wrapped inside. You can make a packed meal special, too. When packing a lunch for someone else, tuck in a surprise. Both children and grownups like surprises! Here are some things that make the packed lunch interesting:

- Include a brightly-colored paper napkin.
- Add a small package of sunflower seeds.
- Put special stickers on the sandwich wrap.
- Cut sandwiches in fancy shapes.
- Put a riddle on crossword puzzle in the bag to solve while the person eats.
- Add a note that says, "You're someone special!"
- For a child, include paper and a crayon.

You see, the surprise doesn't always have to be something to eat. An unexpected surprise makes a meal more fun to eat.

Let's Make a Packed Lunch

Here's a nutritious lunch menu that you could make:

MENU 1

Lunch to Go!

Ham, Cheese, and Lettuce Sandwich
Orange   Carrot and Celery Sticks
Refrigerator Cookies

Look at the menu. Can you put each food into a food group? As a hint, the sandwich really belongs in several groups. A balanced meal has foods from these four groups: Milk and Cheese; Meat, Poultry, Fish, and Beans; Fruit and Vegetable; and Bread and Cereal. It may even have something from the Fats and Sweets Group for extra flavor and energy.

Making Refrigerator Cookies

1. Choose a store-bought refrigerator dough. This dough is a convenience food. Do you remember what a convenience food is?
2. Read the package instructions carefully.
3. Preheat the oven.
4. Gather the equipment. You will need a cutting board so you won't mark the table or counter. A sharp knife will give thin, even slices. A turner will help you lift cookies off the cookie sheet without spoiling their shape. You will also need a cooling rack.
5. Slice cookies with a knife.
6. Place cookies on the cookie sheet.
7. To bake, put the cookie sheet on the rack in the oven's center. This helps cookies bake evenly.
8. Bake according to directions.
9. Watch the time carefully so the cookies won't burn. When the cookies are done, the bottoms will be slightly browned.
10. Remove the cookie sheet from the oven with potholders.
11. Use the turner to remove cookies from the cookie sheet. Place cookies on a wire rack to cool. Then wrap two or three for lunch. The remaining cookies can be stored in plastic bags for an after-school snack or other lunches. If they won't be used in a couple of days, you can freeze them for several months.

You can buy refrigerator cookie dough in the supermarket. You just need to slice and bake according to directions.

Making a Sandwich

1. Gather your equipment. You'll need a cutting board, small spatula, and a bread knife.
2. Gather the sandwich ingredients. You'll need two bread slices, a ham slice, a cheese slice, one or two lettuce leaves, and two teaspoons of soft butter or margarine.
3. Place bread on the cutting board. Use the spatula to spread one side of each slice with butter or margarine.
4. Put the sandwich together. First, put a ham slice on one slice of bread. Add a slice of cheese and top with lettuce. Then place the other slice of bread, buttered side down, on top.
5. With the bread knife, cut the sandwich in half.
6. Wrap the sandwich. Look at the directions on page 159.

Sandwiches that are going to be carried and not refrigerated should be made without mayonnaise. Use butter or margarine to keep the bread soft. Mayonnaise spoils easily and can make you sick.

Cutting Carrot and Celery Sticks

1. Pick out a crisp, fresh carrot. Choose a fresh stalk of celery.
2. Gather your equipment. You'll need a cutting board, a sharp knife, and a vegetable brush.
3. Scrub the carrot under water with the vegetable brush. Remove all the dirt. Don't peel. The outer layer is a good source of nutrients and fiber. Cut both ends off the carrot.
4. Clean the celery with cold water. Gently rub the dirt off with your fingers. Cut both ends off the celery stalk.
5. Cut the carrot and celery stalk into long, thin strips. Then cut them into pieces about two to three inches long.
6. Wrap the pieces in plastic wrap or place them in a plastic bag. Then refrigerate to keep them crisp.

Preparing an Orange

1. Select a firm, fresh orange.
2. Wash the orange under clean, cold water.
3. Gather your equipment—a cutting board and a utility knife.
4. Use a sharp knife to cut through the peel. Make four cuts from the stem end to the bottom. But don't cut into the fruit. Now it's easy to peel the orange when you're ready to eat it.

Packing Your Lunch Bag

1. Get a clean, fresh lunch bag.
2. Place the orange and the vegetable sticks on the bottom.
3. Put the sandwich in next.
4. Put the cookies on top of the sandwich.
5. Tape milk money to the inside of the bag.
6. Add a clean, paper napkin.
7. Put the edges of the bag together. Fold them down.
8. If you make this lunch at home, refrigerate it until you leave for school.

To give this meal the real test, store it in the refrigerator for a day before you eat it.

Remember to Clean-Up!
Use this checklist for your clean up:

- Did you wash the equipment carefully?
- Was the equipment returned to the right place?
- Did you put away the supplies for wrapping the food?
- Are the crumbs brushed up? Are countertops clean?
- Was the kitchen left neat?

Evaluating a Packed Lunch
Evaluate your packed lunch. Did it look good when you removed it from the bag? Was any food crushed? Did your wrapping keep the food clean and fresh? List the good and bad points of the meal. How would you improve it?

Keeping Foods Safe to Eat

You need to be very careful to keep packed lunches and other carried meals safe to eat. This includes choosing foods that won't spoil and keeping food clean and at the right temperature.

Choose Safe Food
Eating spoiled food can make you sick. Choose foods that don't spoil quickly. Some foods spoil faster than others do. These foods are mixtures of foods with mayonnaise or salad dressing, cream fillings in desserts, fish and many meats, and hard-cooked eggs removed from the shell.

Keep Food Clean
Colds and other illnesses can be spread by germs which grow on food. Germs are tiny living things that are too small to see with your eyes, and they carry disease. You can protect foods from germs and dirt if you:

- always wash your hands before handling food.
- wash the lunch box each time you use it.
- don't put unwrapped food, such as an apple, into a lunch bag you have used before. In fact, use a new, clean bag each time.
- keep food well covered to keep out bugs and dirt.

Keep Cold Food Cold and Hot Food Hot

Foods spoil quickly at room temperature. Below 40°F and above 140°F food stays safe longer and germs on food don't grow as fast. Keeping food hot isn't easy, but there are many ways to keep food cold. Follow these guidelines to keep cold food cold and hot food hot.

- Freeze foods ahead. Put frozen food in the lunch bag or box. When you open your lunch a few hours later, the food will be thawed and safe, too. Remember that fresh fruits and vegetables can't be frozen, so leave the lettuce and tomato off of a sandwich you are going to freeze. Salads and sandwich fillings made with mayonnaise can't be frozen either.
- Refrigerate your packed lunch or picnic foods at home as long as you can.
- Keep foods that spoil away from heat or sunlight.
- Use *insulated containers* to protect food from cold or heat for a short time. An ice chest or a vacuum bottle is insulated. A lunch bag isn't.
- Bring hot drinks and soup in a vacuum bottle. A vacuum bottle can be used for cold fruit juice or milk, too.
- If you plan to eat a hot picnic dish right away, cook it at home first. Cover, then wrap it in layers of newspaper. To keep it hot store the container of food in a cooler without ice until you eat.
- Keep your lunch box cold with a *chemical cold pack* which freezes colder than ice. You can buy one of these in a store. Freeze it for 24 hours before using it. In an ice cooler, you can also use ice. Freeze ice in a plastic container or plastic bag.

An insulated container such as this can be used to keep hot foods hot or cold foods cold.

CHAPTER REVIEW

Summary

A packed lunch should be appealing, nutritious, and safe to eat. It can include many different foods from the four main food groups.

Sandwiches are popular packed lunch foods because they're easy to carry and eat. Sandwiches can be made with many different breads, fillings, and spreads. They contain ingredients from several food groups. Raw vegetables and fruits are easy to prepare and carry, too. They are good sources of vitamins and fiber, and they are low in calories. Many different cookies are nice for a packed lunch.

Sandwiches must be carefully packed to stay fresh. And all the foods must be packed so they don't get crushed. Surprises in a packed lunch make it special.

A safe packed meal contains foods that don't spoil quickly. The food and containers are kept clean. Cold foods are packed so they stay cold, and hot foods are packed so they stay hot.

What Have You Learned?

1. What are the characteristics of a good packed lunch?
2. How should you prepare fresh fruit and vegetables for a packed lunch?
3. Describe the correct way to pack a lunch box or bag.
4. List five good foods to take to school or on a picnic. List five foods to avoid packing.
5. What might happen if you eat spoiled food?
6. List 3 ways to keep picnic foods cold.

Things to Do

1. Demonstrate to your classmates how to wrap a sandwich.
2. Plan a special surprise for a child's lunch box. Describe it.
3. Make a poster to tell about safe packed lunches for school.
4. Write a menu for a nutritious packed lunch.
5. Choose a fruit that's new to you. Find out more about it—where it grows, what nutrients it has, how to prepare it.

A LIGHT MEAL—LUNCH OR SUPPER

broth	another name for stock
condensed soup	convenience soup with some water removed; needs to have liquid added in cooking
dehydrated soup	convenience dry soup; needs water added
dressing	sauce added to salads to add flavor
leftovers	foods not eaten at a previous meal
salad	mixture of two or more foods most often made with different types of vegetables or fruit
soup	food made primarily with liquid
stock	liquid left after cooking meat, poultry, or fish in water
thaw	to bring something frozen to room temperature
yeast	ingredient used to make dough rise

After reading this chapter, you should be able to:

- make a convenience soup.
- describe the ingredients in three different salads.
- explain how to care for salad greens.
- explain the difference between yeast and quick breads.
- list the steps in making a hot sandwich.
- prepare and serve a light meal.

W hat do you like for lunch or supper? If you are like many people you want a light, quick meal. Perhaps pizza, salad, or the all-American hamburger sound good. What are your favorites?

Most people don't eat three big meals each day. A light meal is a good way to get nutrients without too many calories. Dinner, either at noon or in the evening, is the big meal of the day.

Like other meals, a good lunch or supper has foods from the four main food groups. As a result, it provides nutrients you need to stay healthy.

What Is a Light Meal?

Light meals are often quick meals. That's what you need when you're busy. Foods that are quick to make include:

- foods that cook fast, such as hamburgers, hot dogs, and eggs.
- foods that don't need cooking. You may like carrot sticks, a tossed salad, or sliced fruit.
- convenience foods that are canned or frozen. For a quick meal, make soup from a can, used canned tuna fish in a salad, or a frozen pizza.

Soup—It's Good Food

Soup is mostly liquid, but it may have other ingredients, too. On a cold day, a hot soup like vegetable soup tastes good with a sandwich. Did you know that some soups are served cold? These are refreshing on a hot day. Find a recipe for a cold fruit soup.

Soups can be very nutritious. They often include foods from all four main food groups. Water is an important nutrient in soup, too. The other nutrients in soup depend on the ingredients.

Soups are either clear or creamy. In a clear soup, you see the ingredients in the bottom of the bowl. Clear soups are made from stock. *Stock* is the liquid left when meat, poultry, or fish is cooked in water. Vegetables are often cooked in this water, too. These foods give flavor and nutrients to the stock. *Broth* is another name for stock.

Soup can be a light meal in itself or it can be served with other foods. Soups, made from a variety of foods, are nutritious.

Creamy soups usually are thickened with flour. You can't see through these soups. You start by making a thin sauce of flour, butter or margarine, and liquid. The liquid may be stock or milk. Then you add other ingredients such as fish, chicken, or vegetables.

Homemade soups are delicious and also can be a money saver. Only small amounts of foods are needed to make a big pot of soup. You also can make soup from leftovers. *Leftovers* are foods not eaten at a previous meal. Using leftover foods also saves you money because the excess food can be used in making other meals instead of being wasted. For fast meals, keep convenience soups handy. They are canned, frozen, or dehydrated.

Some canned and frozen soups just need reheating. You can do this in a saucepan on your range or in a microwave oven. Other canned and frozen soups are condensed. *Condensed* soups, such as canned tomato soup, had some water removed when they were made so you will need to add water or milk before heating them. You will find directions on the can.

Dehydrated soups are dry soups. They have had all the water removed. You add liquid, then heat. Instant soups are even easier to make. You put the instant soup mix in a bowl. Then add boiling water as directed on the package and the soup is ready!

There are many varieties of condensed soup to choose from. Remember to add water or milk according to the directions on the can.

You can make soups special by:

- mixing two kinds of canned soup together. For example, tomato soup and cheddar cheese soup taste good together. If these are condensed soups, remember to add the liquid!
- adding leftovers to soup. Blend chopped meat or chicken into vegetable soup. Or add cooked vegetables to chicken noodle soup.
- sprinkling toppings on soup just before you serve them. Grated cheese is good. Can you think of others?

Canned soups can be made more interesting by adding other ingredients. Explore some of these possibilities. You just might like them.

You don't have to go to a restaurant for a good salad. You can create your own. Select items from this list:
- Lettuce leaves ■ Tomato wedges ■ Chopped mushrooms
- Green pepper circles
- Carrot circles ■ Bread cubes
- Ham cubes ■ Leftover cooked peas ■ Spinach leaves
- Sliced cucumbers ■ Bean sprouts ■ Chopped olives
- Sliced onions ■ Chopped bacon ■ Grated cheese
- Leftover cooked green beans

Salad-Making

Soup and salad make a perfect combination for a light meal. A *salad* is generally a mixture of different types of vegetables or fruit. Salad ingredients usually are tossed with a dressing. A *dressing*, which is like a sauce, adds flavor to the salad. Familiar examples are French and Italian salad dressings.

A salad is good with any meal. For lunch or supper, serve salad with soup or a sandwich. Or serve salad as the main dish. For a hearty dinner, serve a small salad with a main dish.

These are some common salads:

- A tossed salad is made with lettuce and sometimes other greens. Tomato, cucumber, and many other chopped raw vegetables may be tossed with the lettuce, too. The dressing is spooned on top or tossed lightly with the vegetables, just before serving.
- There are many good vegetable salads. Coleslaw is made with shredded cabbage, shredded carrot, and mayonnaise. Potato salad tastes good with hot dogs.
- A fruit salad may combine many different fruits. Fruit may be chopped or sliced with fruit juice poured over it. A fruit cocktail is an example of this type of salad. You can make your own fruit cocktail or buy it in a can. A Waldorf salad is another fruit salad. It combines chopped apples, chopped celery, and chopped nuts. Then it is blended with mayonnaise and sometimes whipped cream.
- A main dish salad is made with a protein food. Remember, you need protein to help your body grow and repair itself. Meat, chicken, fish, eggs, or cheese are high in protein. Both chicken and tuna salad are main dish salads.
- Molded salads are made with gelatin and chilled. As the gelatin sets, the salad takes on the shape of the container or mold in which it is placed. You can make a molded salad with fruit-flavored gelatin. First, dissolve the gelatin in hot liquid. Then add other ingredients such as chopped fruit and additional liquid. Pour the mixture into a mold. Refrigerate several hours or overnight until it sets.

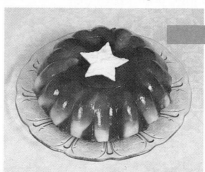

This molded salad was made from gelatin. It should be made the day before it is served so it will have time to set.

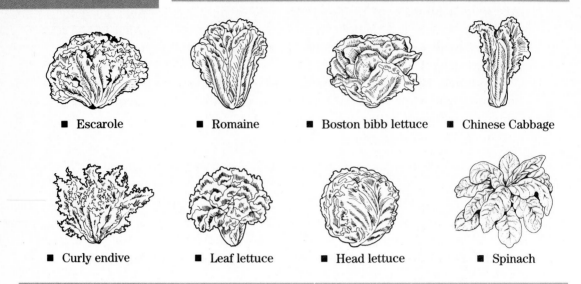

■ Escarole ■ Romaine ■ Boston bibb lettuce ■ Chinese Cabbage

■ Curly endive ■ Leaf lettuce ■ Head lettuce ■ Spinach

Salad Ingredients Head lettuce is the most popular ingredient in salads. But there are many other fresh salad greens to choose from, too.

By mixing the types of greens, salads are more interesting. Some greens such as parsley and endive have curly leaves. Spinach is dark green, while leaf lettuce may have a purplish-red color on the leaf tips. Bibb lettuce has a mild flavor, and endive is bitter. Next time you go to the supermarket, see what salad greens you find.

For an appealing salad, start with fresh greens. Buy salad greens which are crisp, not wilted. Take them home right away. Salad greens are tender, so handle them carefully to keep them from bruising and becoming discolored. Remove damaged leaves and then rinse the greens under cold, running water. Drain off the water and pat the greens dry with paper towels. Put the greens in a plastic bag or covered container before storing them in the refrigerator.

Variety makes vegetable and main dish salads more interesting. Think of all the ingredients on a restaurant salad bar. It's fun to build your own salad the way you like it.

Salad dressings add flavor. Some dressings are made with oil and vinegar. French and Italian dressings are examples. Others, like Thousand Island and Blue Cheese dressing, are made with mayonnaise. Add the dressing just before you serve a salad. Otherwise, the leaves will wilt. For convenience, stores have many bottled salad dressings. You can also buy dry mixes where you just add vinegar and oil and mix.

Breads—Good with Any Meal!

Bread goes with any meal. Earlier you learned about quick breads that are fast to make. You just combine the ingredients then bake the bread right away.

Yeast breads are another kind of bread. The ingredients are first made into dough. Dough is a thick mixture made of flour and a liquid. Yeast breads contain sugar, yeast, and other ingredients which add flavor. *Yeast* is an ingredient which makes dough rise. As the dough rises, it gets light and airy. This takes an hour or more. Then you shape the dough into rolls or bread loaves, let it rise again, and bake it. It takes a long time to make yeast breads from scratch.

For convenience you can buy frozen yeast dough and save the steps of measuring and mixing ingredients. The dough only needs to thaw and rise. To *thaw* means that something frozen warms to room temperature. After the dough rises, you bake the bread. When you buy frozen dough, follow the package directions carefully.

Most dinner rolls are yeast rolls. You can make them from scratch or buy the convenience forms. Some convenience forms are frozen, while others only need to be heated and browned in the oven. For real time savings, some store-bought rolls can be served without heating.

Bread and dinner rolls taste nice with salads and soups, especially when they are still warm from the oven.

Yeast can be purchased in the refrigerated section of your supermarket. It is used in a wide variety of breads. Because the dough must rise, these breads take a long time to make from scratch.

Sandwiches Served Hot

Sandwiches go well with salads and soups. They can be hot or cold. For variety, serve hot sandwiches, such as a hamburger, a grilled cheese sandwich, or a hot dog. Or you might use meatloaf, leftover chicken, or even a fried egg.

Many forms of breads are used to make sandwiches. Hamburgers, hot dogs, and barbecue sandwiches are often served on soft buns. A hot beef sandwich is good on a hard roll. Grilled cheese sandwiches can be made on white, whole-wheat, or rye bread slices.

Tacos and pizza are hot sandwiches! And both can be very nutritious.

Let's Make a Light Meal

Here are three menus for light meals. They can be prepared quickly. Perhaps you can prepare one or all the menus at school.

MENU 1

Hot Dogs in the Spotlight!

Hot Dog in a Blanket
Peach and Cottage Cheese Salad
Milk

Hot dogs can be boiled or broiled. For something special, you can even bake hot dogs in a yeast dough "blanket."

Cottage cheese goes well with fruit as a salad. Since it is a dairy product, cottage cheese is high in protein, calcium, and riboflavin. Why are these nutrients important?

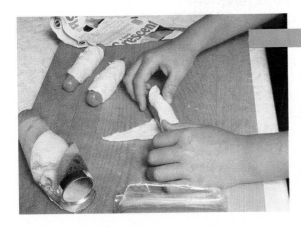

For variety try making "hot dogs in blankets." Place the hot dog on a flat unbaked cresent roll and roll the dough around it. Serve with mustard or catsup.

Preparing Hot Dogs in a Blanket

1. Preheat the oven to 425°F.
2. Gather your equipment. You'll only need a cutting board, a cookie sheet, and potholders.
3. Gather the ingredients. For four people, you'll need four hot dogs. You will also need refrigerator dough for four unbaked crescent rolls. These rolls are convenience yeast breads.
3. Place the unbaked rolls on the cutting board. Unroll them so they are flat and seperate them into four individual pieces of dough.
4. Place the hot dog on the wide end of the dough. Then roll the dough around the hot dog, and place it on a cookie sheet.
5. Most packages of refrigerator crescent rolls have dough for eight rolls. Don't waste the leftovers. Shape the dough into crescents. Bake them with the others.
8. Bake in the oven for 10 to 12 minutes. The rolls will be golden brown. Use potholders to remove the cookie sheet from the oven.

Preparing Peach and Cottage Cheese Salads

1. Gather your equipment. You'll need plates, a spoon, and a can opener.
2. Gather the ingredients to make four salads. You'll need four lettuce leaves, a small carton of cottage cheese, a small can of peach halves, and parsley or mint leaves.
3. Wash and drain the lettuce and then place one leaf on each plate.
4. Open the can of peaches and drain off the juice. Place one peach half on each leaf of lettuce.
5. Spoon cottage cheese into each peach half.
6. Garnish with parsley or mint. Garnish means to decorate one food with another.

A Meal with Burgers!

Hamburger
Carrot-Raisin Salad   **Pickles**
Milk

Hamburgers are the all-time American favorite. You may either broil or fry them. Both methods are fast. A cheeseburger is made like a hamburger with one difference. A slice of cheese is added on top of the hamburger just before it's finished cooking. This adds both flavor and nutrients.

A carrot-raisin salad tastes good with a hot sandwich. Carrots are a good source of vitamin A. Why is this nutrient so important? The pickles and milk are ready to serve. Let's learn to make the salad and hamburgers!

Preparing Carrot-Raisin Salad

1. Gather your equipment. You'll need a vegetable brush, utility knife, cutting board, shredder-grater, bowl, dry measuring cups, a mixing spoon, and four plates or bowls to serve the salad in.
2. Gather your ingredients. To make four servings, you'll need four small carrots, raisins, mayonnaise, and four lettuce leaves.
3. Scrub the carrots under water with the brush.
4. Cut the tops and bottoms off the carrots.
5. Grate the carrots into a bowl.
6. Measure ¼ cup raisins, and pour them into the bowl.
7. Meausre ¼ cup mayonnaise, and spoon it into the bowl.
8. Blend all the ingredients with the spoon.
9. Divide the salad into four portions.
10. Serve each portion on a lettuce leaf which has been placed on an individual plate or in a bowl. Remember to wash the lettuce first, then pat it dry with paper towels.

When grating carrots be very careful as your hand gets closer to the grater. Stop before your fingers touch the grater. It's easy to scrape or cut your fingers.

Preparing hamburgers

1. Gather your equipment. You'll need a frying pan or a broiler pan, a turner, and potholders.
2. Gather your ingredients. You'll need ground beef and hamburger buns. One pound of ground beef makes four hamburgers.
3. Divide one pound of ground beef into four portions. Round each portion into a ball with your hands.
4. To make patties, flatten each ball. Be sure the patties aren't too thin in one place or too thick in another. Make them about four inches wide. They will shrink when cooked.
5. To Broil:
   Place the patties on the broiler pan, put the pan in the broiler and turn the control to "Broil." Cook for about seven minutes. Using potholders, remove the broiler pan from the broiler and turn the patties over with a turner. Put the pan back in the broiler and cook for another seven minutes, or until done. Turn the control to "Off" and remove the patties from the pan with the turner.
6. To Fry:
   Place the patties in a greased frying pan and place the pan on a stove burner. Turn the burner to medium-high heat. Fry the patties seven minutes on one side. Turn the patties with a turner, and cook for seven more minutes, or until done. Turn the burner off and remove the patties from the pan with the turner.
7. Serve the patties while they are hot. Place each patty in a bun. You might add extra ingredients for flavor, nutrition, and color. For example, add a cheese slice, lettuce, or a tomato slice.

Soup and Salad!

Tomato-Cheese Soup
Chef's Salad   Hot Rolls
Apple Juice

This easy menu uses three convenience foods—soup from a can, brown-and serve rolls, and frozen apple juice concentrate.

A chef's salad is like a tossed salad. The extra ingredients are strips of meat and cheese. It is a main dish salad and represents three food groups.

Preparing Brown-and-Serve Rolls

1. Read the package directions. You may bake the rolls right in the package tray or on a cookie sheet.
2. Preheat the oven to the temperature indicated on the package.
3. Bake the rolls according to directions.
4. Serve the rolls while they are hot.

Making a Chef's Salad

1. Gather your equipment. You'll need a bowl, measuring spoons, a spoon and fork for mixing, cutting board, and a utility knife.
2. Gather the ingredients. To make one salad, you'll need: ¼ of a small head of lettuce, a small tomato, ¼ cucumber, cheese slice, ham slice, and 2 tablespoons salad dressing.
3. Wash and drain the vegetables.
4. Break the cleaned and drained lettuce into small pieces and place in the bowl.
5. On the cutting board, cut the tomato into wedges. Slice the cucumber. Add the tomato and cucumber to the bowl with the lettuce.
6. Slice the cheese and ham into strips and add them to the contents of the bowl.
7. Keep the salad chilled until you're ready to serve it.
8. Pour the salad dressing over the other ingredients. Carefully toss with the spoon and fork.

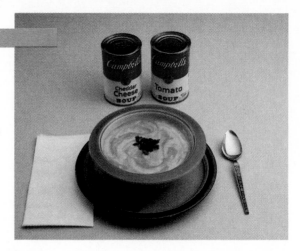

Canned soups can also be made more interesting by combining two different kinds, such as cheese and tomato. Cut parsley on top makes an attractive garnish.

Preparing Tomato-Cheese Soup

1. Gather your equipment. You'll need a saucepan, wooden spoon, ladle, can opener, and kitchen shears.
2. Gather the ingredients. You will need a can of cheese soup, a can of tomato soup, water, and fresh parsley. Two cans of soup will feed three to four people.
3. Open the soup cans. Pour them into the saucepan.
4. Add two cans of water to the saucepan.
5. Stir the soup and water with a wooden spoon until they are well blended.
6. Warm the soup on the stove over medium heat.
7. When the soup is hot, turn off the heat. Use a ladle to pour the soup into bowls.
8. Snip parsley with your kitchen shears. Sprinkle the parsley on the soup for extra color!

Serving, Cleaning, and Evaluating

Does a quick, light meal need to be attractive? If it is, it's even more enjoyable. Adding a garnish, such as parsley, makes the meal more interesting and colorful. These extra touches seem to make the food taste better. What other garnishes can you think of?

Serve this meal like any other. Write down the dishes and flatware you'll need to serve your menu. Now set the table with placemats or a tablecloth, napkins, flatware, and the proper dishes.

Clean up properly after your meal. Make a checklist for cleanup and then follow it. Evaluating your menu is a good idea, too. Did the meal look good? Was the menu nutritious? Did it taste good?

CHAPTER REVIEW

Summary

Lunch and supper are light meals compared to dinner which is the big meal of the day. Sandwiches, soups, and salads are good foods for light meals.

Ingredients from all four main food groups can be used to make soup. Store-bought convenience soups such as canned, frozen, condensed, and dehydrated soups are easy to make.

Salads can be the main dish or a side dish. They are made with vegetables, fruit, and other ingredients. Salad greens must be carefully handled so they stay fresh.

Yeast breads are often served with soups and salads. There are several convenience forms of yeast breads which you can buy so you can prepare yeast bread or rolls quickly.

What Have You Learned?

1. What is the difference between a light supper and dinner?
2. How do you make a canned soup? Dehydrated soup?
3. What ingredients might you use in a tossed salad?
4. How would you take care of salad ingredients before making the salad?
5. Explain why yeast breads take longer to make than quick breads.
6. Describe two ways of cooking a meat patty.
7. How could you make a convenience soup special?
8. Look at the three menus in this chapter. Evaluate the menus using the Daily Food Guide.
9. How could you make a light meal look nice?

Things to Do

1. List three soups you can buy. For each one, describe two ways to make the soup special.
2. Make a poster with magazine pictures. Show all the different breads you might serve with a soup or salad.
3. Write a menu for a lunch you might eat at home. Be sure your menu is nutritionally balanced.

DINNERS FOR SPEED AND CONVENIENCE

casserole	one-dish meal, cooked and served in a baking dish
converted rice	rice that is partly cooked then dried
instant rice	rice that is cooked and dried
microwave cooking	fast way to cook; done in a microwave oven
pasta	food made with flour and water
sauce	liquid mixture used to flavor foods
saute	to fry lightly and quickly
stir-fry	to cook thinly-sliced food quickly in a small amount of hot fat
strain	to remove liquid from food with a utensil that has holes
wok	frying pan used to stir-fry

CHAPTER 11

After reading this chapter, you should be able to:

- *explain the benefits of a one-dish meal.*
- *describe how to cook pasta.*
- *list three ways to serve rice.*
- *state two benefits of stir-fry cooking.*
- *demonstrate how to reheat leftovers in a microwave oven.*
- *prepare a quick dinner meal.*

I

n a hurry? It seems that many people want fast meals. Some have after-school meetings or practices, while others have busy work schedules. Or maybe they want to spend time with friends or a favorite hobby. You may have a busy schedule, too. A schedule lists the things you do with your time.

Busy people often want ways to prepare meals quickly. Even if you're in a hurry, you need to eat nutritious meals to stay healthy. It takes planning.

Cooking a One-Dish Meal

One-dish meals save time and energy because you spend time on one recipe, not several. You can prepare ahead and use fewer dishes, so clean-up is faster. One-dish meals can be very nutritious. The main ingredient is usually high in protein. Meat, chicken, fish, eggs, or cheese may be the main ingredient. Why do you need protein?

Another ingredient is generally high in carbohydrate. This might be pasta or rice. Vegetables are often a part of the recipe, too. Can you see how a one-dish meal could include foods from all four main food groups?

Casseroles and stews can be one-dish meals. Does your family have favorite one-dish meals? To make them more interesting, serve salad or bread on the side.

Casseroles provide nutritious meals for busy times.

Casseroles to Make Ahead

Casseroles are cooked and served in a baking dish. They may also be a one-dish meal. Casseroles save you time and energy. You can prepare one the night before, refrigerate it, then cook it the next day.

A casserole is really a mixture of several ingredients. Tuna-noodle casserole is a popular one. It's made from canned tuna, noodles, chopped celery, and a sauce. A sauce is a thick mixture made with some kind of flavorful liquid. Tomato sauce and barbecue sauce are examples.

Cookbooks list many casseroles. When you bake macaroni and cheese in the oven, it's really a casserole. Add chopped ham and tomato, and you have included foods from each of the four main food groups.

Pasta for Dinner

"Pasta" might be a new word to you. But you may already know many kinds of pasta. Spaghetti, macaroni, and noodles are three kinds. Can you name others? *Pasta* is made with flour and water. That means it's a grain product. What food group does pasta belong in? You're right if you said the Bread and Cereal Group.

Pasta is a good source of carbohydrate which gives you energy. See if the word "enriched" is on the package. If so, the pasta is also a good source of B vitamins and iron. Chapter 2 explains why these nutrients are important.

Storing and Cooking Pasta   Pasta breaks easily, so buy a package that isn't damaged and handle it carefully. Keep pasta in a cool, dry place. After you open the package, keep it in a tightly-covered container. This also helps keep it clean.

Pasta must be cooked in boiling water or it won't be soft enough to eat. Even if pasta is part of a casserole, you must cook it first. The chart on page 188, "Cooking Pasta," tells you how. Beware! Pasta doubles in sizes when cooked, so cook it in a big pan. Don't make more than you need.

 Measure water and salt into a large pot. Use 2 quarts (8 cups) water and 1 tablespoon salt for every 8 ounces (1/2 pound) pasta.

 Bring the water to a boil.

 Add 1 teaspoon of cooking oil to the water. This helps stop water from boiling over. It also helps keep pasta from sticking together.

 Add the pasta slowly to the water. The water should continue to boil. If it stops, the pasta might stick together.

 Stir the pasta from time to time. This also helps keep it from sticking. Cook the pasta only until it's tender. It should't be soft or mushy. The package directions will tell you how long.

 Pour pasta into a strainer to drain. Don't rinse the pasta with water.

Ways to Serve Pasta Think of all the different ways you can serve pasta for dinner.

- Spaghetti with meat sauce is very popular.
- Macaroni and cheese is good for lunch or dinner.
- Pasta is part of many casseroles. Lasagna, an Italian recipe, is one example. Tuna noodle casserole is another.
- Noodles taste good in soup. You may like chicken-noodle soup.
- Cold macaroni blends well with salad ingredients. Mix it with cooked, cold vegetables and mayonnaise. Add chicken or ham and it becomes a main-dish salad.

Pasta is used in many dishes. Spaghetti and meatballs, macaroni and cheese, lasagne, and chicken noodle soup are four examples.

One-Dish Meals with Rice

In some ways, rice is like pasta. It is a grain product so it belongs in the Bread and Cereal Group. The nutrients are similar and it blends with many foods.

Enriched rice is nutritious. As you read in chapter 7, enriched means that vitamins and minerals lost in the refining process have been replaced. Look for the word enriched on the package when you shop. Enriched rice is a good source of B vitamins and iron.

There are different kinds of rice. White rice is generally sold in plastic bags. Converted rice and instant rice usually are sold in boxes. *Converted rice* is partly cooked. And *instant rice* is already cooked and dried. You can prepare both quickly at home. You'll also find other kinds of rice at the store.

Rice is sold in different forms: white rice, converted rice, and instant rice. In addition many varieties of flavored rice are available.

Storing and Cooking Rice   Take care of rice just like pasta. Keep it in a cool, dry place. After you open the package, put rice in a tightly-covered container.

Rice also needs to be cooked before you eat it. Different kinds of rice are cooked in different ways. The cooking time changes too, so read the directions on the package. To make rice light and fluffy, don't stir it too much because stirring makes it sticky. Don't rinse rice either. Some of the nutrients will go right down the drain!

Rice is good in many recipes. Serve rice with butter and seasonings, or combine it with meat and vegetables for a one-dish meal. Rice makes more expensive ingredients go farther. Although it may sound funny, we say that rice "stretches" the meat!

Ways to Serve Rice   These are some common ways to serve rice:

- Chinese dishes taste good on rice. For example, serve chop suey on rice.
- Many recipes with sauce are served over rice. A sauce gives flavor to a recipe. Creamed tuna and beef stroganoff are made with sauces and are served over rice.
- Many casseroles are made with rice. Rice is convenient because it can be cooked in the oven.
- Seasoned rice is often served with Mexican foods, such as enchiladas.
- Rice can be cooked, then chilled. Then you can mix it with salad ingredients. By adding meat, chicken, or fish, it becomes a main-dish salad.
- Seasoned rice is good to serve with chicken or fish.

Cooking to Save Time

Some cooking methods are faster than others. Broiling, for example, is faster than baking. And frying is faster than roasting. Two other cooking methods are fast. These are stir-frying and microwave cooking. Using leftovers can be another timesaver.

Stir-Fry Cooking

To *stir-fry* is to cook thinly-sliced food quickly in a small amount of hot fat. To be sure the food cooks evenly, stir constantly.

Stir-frying is new to American cooking, but Oriental people have cooked this way for many years. Stir-frying is popular because it is a fast, nutritious way to cook. Stir-fried vegetables are especially good. They stay colorful and crunchy.

Stir-frying is fast, but you need time to get the food ready. Slice meat and vegetables very thin and in pieces of equal size. You may also chop the ingredients.

Stir-frying is often done in a wok. A *wok* is a special kind of frying pan. It is wide at the top and narrow at the bottom. This allows for a heavy concentration of heat at the bottom of the wok. You can also use any frying pan to stir-fry.

To serve more people at very little added cost, toss cooked rice with stir-fried foods.

Stir-frying is often done in a wok, but it doesn't have to be. An electric fry pan works well too.

When cooking in a microwave oven be sure to follow directions carefully. And only use utensils that are microwave safe such as those shown here.

Microwave Cooking

Microwave cooking is another fast way to cook! For many foods, it is quicker than cooking with a range. A microwave oven is also good for reheating and cooking vegetables only until they're tender but crisp.

Cooking in a microwave oven is different from cooking with a range. The cooking utensils are different, the timing is different, and some methods are different.

Many pots and pans are metal. You can't use these in a microwave oven because metal damages the oven. Instead, use these containers:

- heat-resistant glass pans, bowls, and measuring cups
- paper plates and bowls (Never use paper in a regular oven!)
- microwave plastics
- plastic cooking bags

The best way to know the cooking time is to check a microwave cookbook. The reason is this. The more food you cook, the longer it takes. Because foods cook so fast, it's easy to overcook.

Rules for Microwave Cooking   These are some tips for preparing food in a microwave oven:

- Never turn the oven on when it's empty. You'll damage it.
- Never use metal containers in the oven.
- Set the oven for the right power. On the range you turn the burner to low, medium, and high. You do the same thing for a microwave oven. When it's on high, or full power, it cooks the fastest. Some foods cook best with less power.
- Be very careful to set the cooking time properly. Some foods cook for only a few seconds!
- Cook in round containers, if possible. Food often overcooks in the corners of a square pan.
- Food cooks slowest in the center. Cook food in a ring shape when you can, or stir food part way through cooking. Stir from the outside in. Your teacher will show you how to do this.
- Cover food to keep it from drying out or splattering. Use paper towels or a glass cover. Plastic wrap is good, too, with one rule. Make a small hole in the plastic with a knife. Then the plastic wrap won't burst.
- Cut pieces of food to about the same size and shape. Then they'll cook in about the same time.
- Help food cook evenly. Turn the dish. Your teacher will show you how to do this, too. Some microwave ovens turn the dish for you.

CREATIVE USES FOR LEFTOVERS

Cooked Ham
- Chop ham, and mix into scrambled eggs.
- Cut ham into strips. Mix into a chef's salad.
- Dice for a ham salad.

Meat Sauce from Spaghetti
- Serve heated sauce on a hamburger roll. Then it's called a "sloppy joe."
- Spoon heated sauce over a baked potato. Top with cheese.
- Spoon heated sauce into a taco shell. Top with chopped lettuce and tomatoes and grated cheese.

Chopped, Cooked Vegetables
- Add vegetables to soup.
- Add vegetables to a tossed salad. Vegetables should be chilled.
- Mix vegetables into a filling for quiche. Quiche is a French dish. It's a pie you serve as a main dish. The filling is made from milk and cheese.

Planning for Leftovers

Leftovers are sometimes called plan-overs. Can you guess why? Remember that leftovers are foods left from a previous meal. They are foods which were never served on a person's plate. To save cooking time later, plan for leftovers.

Leftovers save you time and energy. You make more food than you will need for one meal. Then store the extra food carefully to keep it safe and good to eat.

Storing Leftovers Safely   Handle leftovers carefully so they don't spoil. Earlier, you learned that spoiled foods can make you sick.

- Keep leftover cooked foods cold. This includes meat, poultry, fish, and vegetables. Store them in the refrigerator. Or freeze them if you don't plan to eat them in three to four days.
- Don't let leftovers sit on the counter. Germs grow best at room temperature. Refrigerate leftover foods as soon as possible after the meal has been served.
- Store leftovers in covered containers so they don't dry out or get dirty. You can cover containers with plastic wrap or foil.
- Store leftovers in small containers. Then they won't take up too much room in the refrigerator.

Left over turkey and other meats must be stored in the refrigerator to keep them safe for eating. If there is no room in the refrigerator you could store them in the garage as long as the temperature is below 40°F.

Reheating Food   You can reheat leftovers in the microwave oven or on the stove. To reheat food in a microwave oven:

1. Place leftover food on a microwave-safe dish.
2. Cover the dish of food with plastic wrap. Poke a small hole in the plastic.
3. Check a cookbook for the power setting and the cooking time.
4. Heat the food according to the directions. This usually takes a very short time.
5. To make the food look freshly cooked, add a new garnish. A parsley sprig or lemon slice might be nice. Or sprinkle with a seasoning such as paprika.

Reheating is one way to serve leftovers. Another way is to serve these foods in other recipes. The chart on page 194, "Creative Uses of Leftovers," will give you some ideas. What other ideas might you add?

Let's Cook a One-Dish Meal

These two menus are fast to prepare. The reason is this. The casserole or skillet dinner is almost a meal in itself. Perhaps you can make one or both menus in school. For extra practice, prepare them for your family.

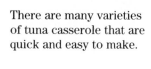

There are many varieties of tuna casserole that are quick and easy to make.

Easy Casserole Dinner

Crunchy-Topped Tuna Casserole
Tossed Salad
Hot Dinner Rolls
Milk

This is an easy casserole dinner. Check the menu, and you'll see that it is a nutritious meal. You can follow the directions for making the casserole and for heating the rolls. Earlier, you learned how to make a tossed salad. It's like a chef's salad without the meat and cheese.

This casserole will serve four people. Make enough salad and rolls for four people, too.

Planning is an important part of cooking. Earlier, you learned to dovetail your cooking tasks. Dovetailing is a way of saving time by fitting tasks together so that you accomplish more than one thing at a time. Look at the menu above. How could you dovetail your tasks?

- While the noodles cook, mix the other casserole ingredients.
- Put the casserole in the oven. While it bakes, prepare the salad, set the table, pour the milk, and get the rolls ready to heat in the microwave oven. At the last minute, turn on the microwave oven. Then the rolls will be hot when served.

Preparing a Tuna Noodle Casserole

1. Gather your equipment. You'll need measuring cups and spoons, a can opener, large saucepan with a lid, small saucepan with a lid, strainer, bowl, 2-quart casserole dish, rubber scraper, mixing spoon, and pot-holders.
2. Gather your ingredients. You'll need water, salt, vegetable oil, medium sized noodles, condensed cheddar cheese soup, milk, tuna, frozen peas, and crackers.
3. Preheat the oven to 350° F.
4. Read the directions for cooking pasta on page 188. Cook four ounces of noodles for the casserole. Drain them.
5. Cook the frozen peas according to the directions on the package.
6. Pour one ten-ounce can of cheese soup into the casserole dish. Use the rubber scraper to remove all the soup from the can.

7. Measure ½ cup milk. Stir the milk into the soup.
8. Strain the tuna in an eight-ounce can. To *strain* is to remove liquid from food with a utensil that has holes. Use a strainer over a bowl. Put the strained tuna into the casserole dish. Throw the fluid from the tuna away. (Rinse the tuna in the strainer first if it was packed in oil, then strain off the water.)
9. Add the cooked frozen peas to the casserole dish, too.
10. Stir the soup, milk, tuna, and peas. They should be well mixed.
11. Blend the cooked noodles into the tuna mixture. Be gentle. You don't want to break the noodles.
12. Crush the crackers. Measure 1 cup. Sprinkle them on the casserole.
13. Bake the casserole in the oven. It will take about 45 minutes to cook. If you make this in class, prepare and bake the casserole on one day. Your teacher will take it out of the oven for you. Reheat and serve it on the next day.

A strainer makes the task of draining off liquid from a food easy.

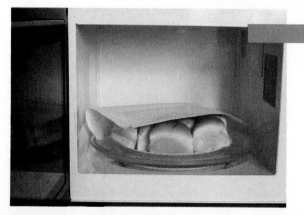

To heat rolls in a microwave oven cover them with a paper towel.

To Heat Rolls in the Microwave Oven:

1. Arrange four dinner rolls on a microwave-safe container.
2. Cover with a paper towel. (When you want to heat just one roll, wrap it in a paper towel.)
3. Set the power on medium-low. Your teacher will show you how.
4. Set the timer for 30 seconds and start the oven. (Heat one roll for just 15 seconds.)
5. Check the rolls before you add more heating time. Overheated breads and rolls get tough and hard in a microwave oven.

MENU 2

A Meal in a Skillet

Beef-Rice Skillet
Sliced Pineapple on Lettuce
Ice Cream
Milk

This is another quick menu. The main dish is made with rice, not pasta. It is made on top of the range, not in the oven. This menu also has a dessert.

This menu is quick because the meat and rice are cooked at the same time, and the salad can be prepared quickly. The dessert is already made. You just need to remove it from the carton and place it in individual bowls.

Once again, evaluate the menu with the food main groups. Good menus follow the main food group guidelines.

Making Beef Rice Skillet

1. Gather your equipment. You'll need a large frying pan and cover, cutting board, paring knife, can opener, measuring cups and spoons, bowl, wooden spoon, and rubber scraper.
2. Gather your ingredients. You'll need cooking oil, onion, raw ground beef, enriched rice, a small can of tomato paste, water, salt, and pepper.
3. Chop one medium-sized onion on the cutting board.
4. Measure 2 tablespoons of oil into the frying pan. Heat the oil. Then add the chopped onion. Cook the onion until it turns clear. Stir the onions while cooking so they don't burn. When you cook onions this way, you saute them. To *saute* means to fry lightly and quickly.
5. Add one-half pound ground beef to the onion in the frying pan. With your wooden spoon, break the meat apart in the pan. Fry it until it gets brown. Again, be sure to stir the meat and onions while cooking.
6. Measure 3 cups of water. Pour it into a bowl. If you want more flavor, use beef broth instead of water. Earlier, you learned that broth was a kind of soup. You can buy broth in a can.
7. Add tomato paste to the water. You'll need the rubber scraper to clean out the can. Blend the water and tomato paste well.
8. Pour the tomato paste and water mixture into the frying pan.
9. Measure 1 cup of uncooked enriched rice. Add it to the frying pan, too.
10. Measure just a little salt and pepper to season it just as you like it. One-half teaspoon of salt should be enough. Use about ¼ teaspoon of pepper.
11. Put the cover on the frying pan. Cook over low heat. Now the food is simmering.
12. The food should be done in about 20 minutes. When the water is absorbed, the rice is done.

Use a wooden spoon to break apart gound beef as you fry it.

Preparing the Salad:

1. Gather the utensils. You will need a can opener, a fork, a teaspoon, and four individual salad plates.
2. Gather the ingredients. You'll need lettuce leaves, a small can of pineapple slices, and salad dressing or mayonnaise.
3. Wash and drain the lettuce leaves. Put one lettuce leaf on each plate.
4. Open the pineapple, and place a slice on top of each lettuce leaf.
5. Refrigerate.
6. When ready to serve, top wtih salad dressing and maybe a cherry for color.

Serving and Cleaning Up Fast

Some people think that setting a pretty table isn't important when they're in a hurry. But making a table look nice doesn't take much time. A fruit bowl or a plant is an easy centerpiece. If you dovetail your mealtime tasks, you can usually set the table while food is cooking. When you're in a rush, these are some ways to save clean-up time.

- Use placemats instead of a tablecloth. The placemats may be paper or plastic.
- Serve food on the plates instead of in serving dishes to save on dish washing.
- Use attractive paper plates if you're in a big hurry.
- Use paper napkins.

Even when you're hurrying, it's smart to evaluate the meal. You might think of more ways to save time!

Everytime you cook, ask yourself how you could improve. This is evaluating your performance.

CHAPTER REVIEW

Summary

One-dish meals, such as casseroles, can be nutritious and timesaving. Pasta and rice are part of many one-dish meals.

Pasta and rice are from the Bread and Cereal Group. They must be stored in a clean dry place and cooked before they're eaten.

Two cooking methods which save time are stir-frying and microwave cooking. Microwave cooking requires a different oven, utensils, and methods than regular cooking.

Planned leftovers must be stored properly to keep them safe to eat. They can be used to save cooking time later.

What Have You Learned?

1. What are the benefits of a one-dish meal?
2. How should you cook pasta?
3. What are three ways to serve rice?
4. What does "enriched" mean?
5. How do you stir-fry vegetables?
6. What are the benefits of stir-fry cooking?
7. Give four rules of microwave cooking.
8. Give three ways you might use leftover vegetables.
9. List three rules for storing leftovers.
10. What are three ways you can save food-preparation time?

Things to Do

1. Give an example of a one-dish meal. Then classify it into the food groups.
2. Look in a cookbook. Find three recipes which use pasta. Also, find three recipes which use rice, and share them with your class.
3. Create a classroom display. In your classroom kitchen show the utensils which are microwave safe.
4. Make a poster to hang in your class showing one or more rules for cooking in a microwave oven.
5. Find magazine pictures of one-dish meals.

DINNER—A LEISURELY MEAL

appetizer	food that starts a meal and is served before the main dish
braise	to cook meat or poultry slowly in a small amount of liquid in a covered pan
cuts of meat	small pieces of meat people buy
dessert	last food served at a meal, usually sweet
dinner	largest meal of the day; it may be in the evening or at midday.
dry heat	cooking with no liquid
family style	a method of serving where the food for several people is put in serving dishes and passed around the table
moist heat	cooking with liquid
poultry	chicken, turkey, or other birds sold as food
roast	to cook uncovered in an oven without liquid
steam	to cook covered over boiling water
stew	to simmer food covered with liquid

After reading this chapter, you should be able to:

- *explain the difference between dry-heat and moist-heat methods of cooking.*
- *explain how to store meat, poultry, and fish.*
- *describe two ways to cook vegetables.*
- *cook a family dinner.*
- *serve a meal "family style."*

"D inner is ready." That's pleasant to hear. But the cook says it's even nicer to hear, "Oh, that was a good dinner."

Once you prepare a family dinner, you'll know why cooks like to have people say, "It's good." Cooking takes time. You need to plan well to prepare a family dinner.

Dinner is, for most people, the largest meal of the day. It may be at midday or in the evening. It's a meal when family members often eat with each other.

Dinner is the meal when family members can usually eat together. In many families it is a special time.

What's for Dinner?

The main dish of a dinner menu is usually meat, poultry, or fish. Sometimes, it's a one-dish meal with one of these foods as the main ingredient. Dinner usually includes one or more vegetables to go along with the main dish. A salad is also nice with dinner. You might want dessert, too. To include all four main food groups, you might also serve dinner rolls and milk.

Let's Learn About Meat

Meat comes from animals. The most common meats are beef, pork, veal, and lamb. Beef and veal are from cows and steers. Veal is from a young cow or steer, and beef is from an older one. Pork is the meat from pigs. Ham, bacon, and sausage are meats, too. Ham and bacon are pork. Many types of sausages are made from pork.

Meat is high in protein. It's also a good source of iron, thiamin, and niacin. For a quick review, check chapter 2 to see what these nutrients do.

Meat comes from different animals. Steaks and hamburgers are beef and come from cows.

Pork chops and spareribs are pork and come from pigs.

Lamb chops and leg of lamb come from lamb.

Ham, bacon and sausage are pork. They come from pigs.

There are many different ways to buy meat. Some cuts are less expensive, usually because they are tougher. This is due to the part of the animal they come from.

Buying Meat Meat comes from different parts of the animal. Large sections of meat are cut from the animal, and these are then cut into smaller pieces. We buy the smaller pieces called the *cuts* of meat. The names of these cuts often refer to the part of the animal the meat came from.

Some cuts are tender, and some are tougher, or less tender. The more tender cuts of meat come from an animal's backbone. This meat is tender because there are no hard-working muscles near the backbone. Most steaks, chops, and rib roasts are tender cuts.

Tougher cuts of meat come from parts of the animal that had hard-working muscles. These cuts are just as nutritious as tender cuts. Tougher cuts must be cooked differently from tender cuts. Then they will be tender to eat. Round steaks, chuck roasts, and stew meat are less-tender cuts.

As a rule, tougher cuts of meat don't cost as much as tender cuts. They can save you money. Before you buy meat, know how you plan to cook it so you can buy an appropriate cut.

HOW DO YOU COOK MEAT?

	Cooking Method	Cuts of Meat
Tender Cuts	**Broil:** 1. Place meat on the broiler pan of the oven. 2. Sprinkle meat with seasonings. 3. Place the pan on the oven rack just under the flame. That should be about 4 inches from the flame. 4. Turn the heat control to broil. 5. Broil the meat for about 5 minutes. The meat will be nicely browned. Then turn the meat. 6. Broil it on the other side in the same way. Watch the meat carefully.	Sirloin steak T-bone steak Chops
	Roast: 1. Set the oven at 350°F. 2. Place the meat in the roasting pan. Put the fat side up. 3. Sprinkle with seasonings. 4. Put roasting pan in the oven. The pan should be in the middle of the oven. 5. Roast for about 20 minutes per pound of meat.	Rib roast
Less Tender Cuts	**Braise:** 1. Place meat in a casserole dish or some other oven-proof container with a cover. 2. Add other ingredients, including a liquid. Cover the cooking utensil. 3. Set oven on 325°F. 4. Place utensil in the middle of oven. 5. Cook for two or more hours. The meal will be very tender.	Round steak Chuck roast
	Stew: 1. Heat a small amount of oil in a frying pan. 2. Brown meat in the pan. 3. Place meat in a saucepan. 4. Add other ingredients and enough water to cover all the food. Cover the saucepan. 5. Simmer the meat until it's very tender.	Stew meat

Look at all the things you can do with ground beef!

- Cook ground beef as patties for hamburgers.

- Make a meat sauce. Serve over spaghetti noodles.

- Combine cooked ground beef with taco (TAH koh) seasonings. Serve in a taco shell as a taco salad with lettuce and tomato.

- Shape uncooked ground beef and other ingredients into a loaf. What do you have? Meatloaf.

- Stuff green peppers with ground beef. Add seasonings. Then bake.

- Add cooked ground beef to macaroni and cheese for a hearty dish.

Cooking Meat Meat is cooked in two ways—with dry heat and with moist heat.

Cooking by *dry heat* means that no liquid is used. Examples of dry heat cooking are roasting, broiling, and baking. You've already learned the definitions of broiling and baking. To *roast* is to cook uncovered in an oven. No liquid is used. Dry heat is used to cook tender cuts of meat.

Cooking with *moist heat* means liquid is used. Meat cooks in water or vegetable juices. Braising and stewing are both methods of cooking by moist heat. To *braise* is to cook meat or poultry slowly in a small amount of liquid in a covered pan. *Stewing* is simmering food covered with liquid. Stews and pot roasts are cooked by moist heat.

The chart on page 209 "How Do You Cook Meat?" will help you learn to cook meats. Usually, meats are cooked at medium temperatures. In the oven, cook meat at 325°F to 350°F. Broiling is the exception because it uses a very high temperature for a short time. When meat cooks in liquid, keep it just below the boiling point—simmer it. Remember, this is cooking by moist heat.

Have you ever been in a restaurant where the waiter asks this question: "Would you like your meat rare, medium, or well-done?" Rare meat is pink on the inside. And it's usually juicier. Well-done meat is well browned. Beef is good any way. Pork must be well-done to be safe to eat.

A roasted chicken is cooked by dry heat.

Let's Learn About Poultry

The word "poultry" may be new to you. *Poultry* includes chicken, turkey, and other birds sold as food. What other poultry can you name? Your answers might include duck and goose.

Like meat, poultry is high in protein. A food high in protein is often the main dish of a meal.

Buying Poultry   Poultry is like meat in other ways. Some poultry is more tender than other kinds. Turkey is usually tender. Chickens that are broiler-fryers are tender, too. But stewing chickens are bigger, older, less tender birds.

Chicken is sold in pieces, as well as whole. For example, you might buy chicken breasts or wings. Chicken legs are often called drumsticks. Usually, pieces cost more per pound than the whole chicken.

If you buy chicken in a package, you may see "broiler" on the label. This means it would be good broiled. But you can cook it in other ways. Some labels say "roasting" or "frying" chicken.

Cooking Poultry   Poultry can be roasted, fried, baked, broiled, or stewed. Because turkey is tender, cook it with dry heat. Roasting is a good way to cook turkey. A broiler-fryer chicken can be fried, baked, or broiled. A tougher stewing chicken must be stewed or braised. Cooking with moist heat at a low temperature for a long time makes it tender.

Chicken, too, can be purchased in different forms. You can buy certain pieces or you can buy the whole chicken.

There are two kinds of fish, some have fins and are called finfish. Trout, red snapper, catfish and perch are examples. Shellfish is the other kind of fish. Lobsters, clams, oysters, and shrimp are examples. They all have a hard shell on the outside.

Let's Learn About Fish

Fish is another nutritious protein food. It's also a good source of minerals, such as iron and iodine. You know that protein is important for the growth and repair of your body. Iron is an important part of your blood. Iodine helps your thyroid gland work properly.

Fish from the ocean is high in iodine. Since ocean water has a lot of salt these fish are called salt-water fish.

Buying Fish   Fish is sold fresh, frozen, and canned. Fresh fish isn't always available. You may have to go to a special store to buy it.

Canned and frozen fish are sold in most grocery stores. For example, tuna is sold in a can. Frozen fish can be thawed and prepared. You can also buy fish as a convenience food, such as fish sticks.

Preparing Fish   Fish can be made into many interesting dishes. You have already made tuna casserole. Fish can also be baked, fried, or broiled. Leftover cooked fish or canned fish is nice in salads. When you add cooked fish to soup, you are really boiling or simmering fish.

Storing Meat, Poultry, and Fish

Because meat, poultry, and fish spoil easily, you must keep them in the refrigerator or freezer. Put them in a covered container or wrap them carefully in freezer paper or plastic bags. Air will dry them out.

In the refrigerator, you can keep meat, poultry, and fish up to three days. Frozen, these foods stay fresh much longer. The sooner you use fish, the better it will taste.

Of course, unopened canned foods are kept on the shelf. Keep them in a cool, dry place.

Let's Learn About Vegetables

Vegetables are excellent sources of vitamins. The Daily Food Guide suggests that you eat vegetables and fruit every day. How many servings do you need?

Dark-green leafy and deep-yellow vegetables are especially high in vitamin A. Remember that vitamin A helps you see in the dark. Some, such as tomatoes and green peppers are good sources of vitamin C. Vegetables are also a good source of fiber. Earlier, you learned that fiber helps your body get rid of waste. Vegetables are also low in calories.

Vegetables can come from different parts of plants—the flower, the leaf, the root, the stem, the fruit, or the seeds. Look at the chart, "Vegetables From Each Part of a Plant, on page 215. You'll see several different vegetables. The chart shows the plant part each vegetable comes from. Many of these vegetables can be eaten raw. Most of them can be cooked in many different ways.

Buying Vegetables When you buy fresh vegetables, be sure they are good quality. Do not buy vegetables that are overly ripe. Good-quality vegetables have:

- a fresh color
- a crispy texture
- no bruises

You can also buy frozen and canned vegetables. They come in different sized packages, and they are sold in a variety of ways. Buy the type that matches your recipes.

Fresh vegetables should be firm, colorful and have no bruises.

VEGETABLES FROM EACH PART OF A PLANT

Part of Plant	Vegetable
Root	Potato Carrot Onion
Stem	Celery Asparagus
Leaf	Spinach Cabbage Lettuce
Flower	Cauliflower Broccoli
Fruit	Tomato Green pepper
Seed	Corn Peas Green beans

A) Peas are seeds.
B) Green peppers are the fruit of the plant.
C) Broccoli is the flower of the plant.
D) Spinach is a leaf.
E) Celery is the stem of the plant.
F) Carrots are roots.

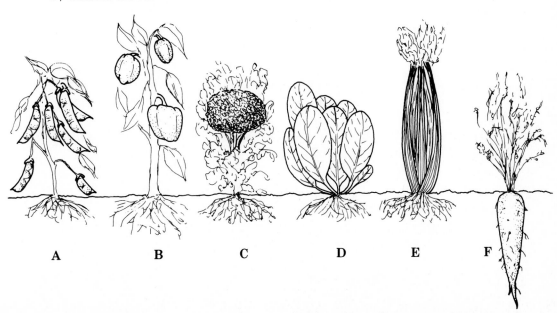

A   B   C   D   E   F

Storing Vegetables   Some vegetables spoil easily. Like meat, you need to refrigerate most fresh vegetables. Putting them in a plastic container or bag before placing them in the refrigerator keeps them from drying out. Or keep them in the vegetable drawer of the refrigerator. Don't refrigerate fresh potatoes, sweet potatoes or onions.

Be sure to use fresh vegetables right away. Even in the refrigerator they can begin to spoil after a week. Frozen vegetables keep much longer. They'll stay good for several months in the freezer. Remember to keep canned vegetables in a cool, dry place!

Cooking Vegetables   Vegetables that are cooked correctly keep their bright color. The nutrients aren't cooked away, and they taste and look very good. These are rules for cooking vegetables:

- Wash vegetables well. Use a vegetable brush.
- Don't peel vegetables if you can eat the skin. For example, don't peel carrots. Potato skins are good, too.
- Don't soak vegetables before cooking them. You'll lose some of the nutrients.
- Cover vegetables when you cook them.
- Cook vegetables in only a small amount of water.
- Don't overcook vegetables. They should be tender but crisp. They shouldn't be mushy.

Vegetables can be cooked in many different ways. Try them simmered, steamed, baked, or cooked in a microwave oven.

To simmer vegetables, cook them in a small amount of water. Remember, simmering is cooking just below the boiling point. Keep them covered. Vegetables should be cooked only until tender but crisp.

To *steam* is to cook, covered, over boiling water. A small vegetable steamer fits in a saucepan. You add water, but the water doesn't touch the steamer. Place the vegetables into the steamer, put on the lid, and turn on the heat.

You can bake vegetables in a casserole or bake them plain. Baked potatoes are simple to cook and good to eat. Squash is also very good when baked.

Vegetables cooked in the microwave oven are delicious! Cut them evenly. Place them on a microwave-safe container. (You don't need water.) Cover the vegetables. Check the cookbook for a power setting and a cooking time. Then start them cooking.

How long do you cook vegetables in a microwave oven? The time depends on:

- the kind of vegetable
- the cooking method
- the size of the vegetables

The important guideline is this. Always cook vegetables as quickly as possible. Check a cookbook to learn the time for each vegetable.

What do you do with the juice left from cooking or from canned vegetables? Add it to soup or gravy. The juice is full of nutrients!

The Dinner Table

Choosing the menu is part of planning a meal. The table setting and the serving are important parts of meal planning too.

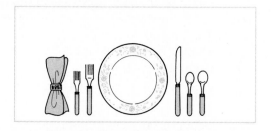

STEPS IN TABLE SETTING

Set a table to fit the menu you are serving.

- Locations of knife, spoons, napkin, and forks.

- Location of bread-and-butter plate.

- Location of salad plate.

- Location of salad plate with bread-and-butter plate.

- Location of drinking glasses.

- Complete place setting.

Setting the Table for Dinner

Setting the table for dinner is like other meals, but you may need more dishes and flatware. That's because you usually have more foods to serve. You may want to use a tablecloth, or you may use matching placemats.

Family style is one way families serve their meals. That means all the food is put on the table in serving dishes. People help themselves. If you serve family style, you'll need serving dishes and utensils.

You already learned how to set a table for brunch. Dinner is the same. You may need an extra fork for salad or dessert. Or maybe you'll need another spoon for dessert. You may also want a special plate for salad.

Serving Dinner and Clearing the Table

It's time to eat when the table is set and when the food's on the table. You can pass serving bowls family style or serve food directly onto the plates in the kitchen.

Clear the table when everyone is done with the main part of the meal. This is the right order:

- First take away the serving dishes and utensils.
- Remove all the dirty dishes and flatware from one person's place. Then go on to the next person.
- Leave cups and saucers if someone wants coffee or tea with dessert. Be sure to leave the dessert fork and coffee spoon.
- Don't stack or scrape dishes at the table. It doesn't look nice.

When food is served family style it is put in serving dishes and passed around the table.

Let's Cook a Family Dinner!

What's for dinner? Baked chicken is easy to prepare and most people like it. You could bake a whole chicken, but in this menu you'll use chicken legs. They bake a little faster.

What goes well with chicken? Cranberry juice is a nice appetizer. An *appetizer* is a food that often starts the meal. It's served before the main dish.

Vegetables are important on a dinner menu. Squash, peas, carrots, or green beans all go well with chicken. If the menu has different colored vegetables, the plate looks nicer. Many people like potatoes with a meal, but there are many interesting vegetables to select from.

This menu has peas and carrots. At home, you might serve a different vegetable. Since the chicken is baked, a good kitchen manager could bake potatoes at the same time. Baked potatoes take an hour in the oven. If you prepare this meal at school, some foods must be prepared the day before. Mashed potatoes would be easier to manage.

A salad is nice for dinner. It adds both nutrients and interest. Even simple salads add a crisp texture to a meal. Coleslaw goes well with chicken or you might prefer a tossed salad or a peach half on lettuce.

This menu doesn't have any bread. You know that a nutritious meal has a serving from the Bread and Cereal Group. So a good dessert might be gingerbread. *Dessert* is the last dish at a meal. Other desserts such as ice cream, cookies, or apple pie go well with a chicken dinner, too.

A dessert baked in the oven is smart planning. Chicken and gingerbread could bake at the same time. And you would save time and money because you use less gas or electricity.

Serve something to drink to complete the meal. Pour milk for teens, children, and adults, too. Adults might also want coffee with their dessert.

Here's the menu that we've planned!

MENU 1

*Chicken
Dinner*

**Cranberry Juice
Baked Chicken Legs
Peas and Carrots   Mashed Potatoes
Gingerbread with Whipped Topping
Milk**

Before making a shopping list check to see what food supplies you already have.

Planning the Meal

Menu planning includes other tasks:

- Check to see what food is on hand, then make a shopping list. Buy the food.
- Make out a time schedule. From each recipe, you will know how long it takes to prepare each food. Then dovetail your work.
- List the equipment you'll need. Be sure you have enough saucepans and other cooking equipment.

Possibly you'll say, "At my house, nobody does all that. We just cook." True, experienced cooks don't write all these things down. They work from habit. And they usually know what's on hand. A beginner has to do things differently. Remember that habits come from doing things over and over.

Some tasks take a longer time. Do these first:

- Clean and place the chicken in the oven to bake.
- Wash, peel, and cut the potatoes, then put them in the pot to simmer.
- Mix the gingerbread, pour it into a pan, and place the pan in the oven with the chicken.

Other tasks take a short time. Do them next.

- Make the coleslaw.
- Cook the peas and carrots.
- Set the table.

Some tasks are even faster. They take only a few minutes each.

- Pour the milk.
- Pour the cranberry juice.

Here is a work plan that is easy for you. Now wash your hands, put on your apron, and go to work!

Baking Chicken

1. Gather your equipment. You'll need paper towels, baking pan, small saucepan, pastry brush, and potholders.
2. Gather your ingredients. You'll need chicken legs (about two per person), butter or margarine, salt, pepper, and paprika.
3. Set the oven for 350°F.
4. Wash the chicken legs and pat them dry with the paper towels.
5. Place the chicken in a shallow baking pan with sides. You don't want the fat to run out into the oven.
6. Melt some butter or margarine in the small saucepan over low heat. Brush a little on the chicken.
7. Sprinkle salt, pepper, and paprika on the chicken.
8. When the oven is hot, put in the chicken legs. Small, tender ones bake in about 45 minutes. Larger ones take about an hour.

Making Mashed Potatoes

1. Gather your equipment. You'll need a vegetable brush, peeler, cutting board, utility knife, saucepan with a cover, fork, strainer, potato masher, and wooden spoon.
2. Gather the ingredients. You'll need one medium or large potato per person, salt, milk, and butter or margarine.
3. Check the potatoes. Be sure there are no bad spots on them. If so, cut the bad spots out.
4. Wash the potatoes with a vegetable brush.
5. Remove the skin with a peeler. Then cut the potatoes in half or quarters on the cutting board.
6. Place the potatoes in the saucepan. Pour water into the pan to just cover the potatoes.
7. Cover and cook over medium heat for 20 to 25 minutes, or until the potatoes are tender when you pierce them with a fork.
8. When the potatoes are cooked, drain them in a strainer. Then return them to the saucepan. Mash until there are no lumps. Add ½ cup milk, 3 tablespoons of butter or margarine, and ¼ teaspoon salt. Beat them with the wooden spoon until they are light and fluffy.
9. Cover the saucepan to keep the potatoes hot.

Making Gingerbread

1. Gather your equipment. You'll need a bowl, a measuring cup, a wooden spoon, a baking pan, a rubber spatula, wax paper, and pot-holders.
2. Gather your ingredients. You'll need a packaged gingerbread mix and other ingredients listed on the package.
3. Read the directions on the package.
4. Grease the pan.
5. Prepare the mix according to the directions and pour into pan.
6. Put the pan in the oven with the chicken.
7. Bake according to the package directions.

MASHING POTATOES

1 Just before you're ready to cook, peel the potatoes, cut them in half and put them into a pan with water. Don't let the potatoes soak in water before cooking or they will lose many of their nutrients.

3 Drain off the water, then mash the potatoes with a potatoe masher.

4 Add milk, butter, seasonings and beat with a wooden spoon until light and fluffy.

2 You can tell if the potatoes are done by piercing them with a fork. If the fork goes into the potatoes easily, they are done.

5 Serve hot.

Preparing Coleslaw

1. Gather your equipment. You'll need a cutting board, utility knife, bowl, apple corer, mixing spoon, and measuring cups and spoons.
2. Gather your ingredients. For four people, you'll need cabbage, an apple, miniature marshmallows, lemon juice, pineapple yogurt, and chopped walnuts.
3. Wash and drain ½ head cabbage. Then cut it into long shreds on the cutting board. Put the cabbage in a bowl.
4. Wash and core the apple, but leave the peel on. Cut it into quarters, then chop into small pieces. Put the apple into the bowl.
5. Measure ⅓ cup chopped walnuts, 1 cup marshmallows, ½ cup pineapple yogurt, and 1 teaspoon lemon juice. Add them to the bowl.
6. Toss the ingredients together with the wooden spoon.
7. Place the salad in the refrigerator until serving time. This will serve four people.

Cole slaw must be stored in the refrigerator or a cooler. Because it contains mayonnaise it will spoil if left at room temperature or in the sun.

Cooking Peas and Carrots

1. Gather your equipment. You'll need a saucepan with a cover and a potholder.
2. Gather your ingredients. You'll need frozen vegetables and water.
3. Take the vegetables from the freezer compartment just before you are ready to cook them.
4. Read the directions on the package. Follow them carefully.
5. Boil a small amount of water in a saucepan.
6. Add the vegetables to the water. Cover the saucepan. Turn the heat down to simmer.
7. Cook as long as the package says to.

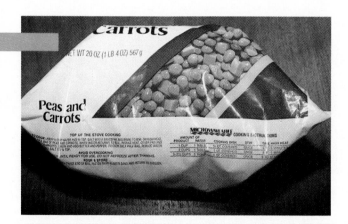

Frozen vegetables can be cooked in the microwave. Just follow the directions on the package.

Setting the Table

1. Choose a tablecloth or placemats.
2. Decorate with a centerpiece.
3. To set the table for each person, you'll need:

   - 1 large plate
   - 1 small plate for salad
   - 1 dinner knife
   - 2 forks, one for the main course and one for dessert
   - 1 spoon
   - 1 napkin
   - 1 glass for milk

4. Gather the serving pieces. You'll need:

   - 1 platter for the chicken
   - 3 serving bowls, for the peas and carrots, the mashed potatoes, and the coleslaw
   - 1 plate for the butter
   - salt and pepper shakers
   - 3 serving spoons for the peas and carrots, the mashed potatoes, and coleslaw
   - 1 fork for the chicken
   - 1 knife for the butter

5. Have juice glasses ready for the cranberry juice.
6. Have dessert plates ready. You can serve the dessert right on individual plates.

If you prepare this meal at school, you will need to prepare some foods the day before. What could be done then? What could be prepared the same day you serve?

Serving, Clearing, and Judging Your Meal

Pour the cranberry juice. Serve the juice first. When everyone is done drinking the juice, clear the glasses. Then serve the main part of the meal.

Fill the plates and bowls with food just before serving time. The salad looks more attractive if you put a leaf of lettuce in the bowl first. For extra color, put fresh parsley on the plate with the chicken and potatoes.

Put the food on the table. Be sure the utensils are next to the serving dishes. Remember to put butter on a plate. A little butter is good on the potatoes. Pour the milk.

When everyone's done with the main part of the meal, clear the table properly.

Serve the dessert on individual plates. If you like, top gingerbread with whipped cream. Pour more milk for anyone who wants it.

"Now, that was a good dinner!" As the cook, you'll be so glad to hear this. But your job isn't over yet. You must still clear the table, wash the dishes, and clean the kitchen. Now judge why the meal was so good!

CHAPTER REVIEW

Summary

Dinner is usually the biggest meal of the day. It may include meat, poultry, or fish, vegetables, a salad, bread, a beverage, and a dessert.

The way meat is cooked depends upon its cut. Tender cuts are cooked with dry heat, and less tender cuts, by moist heat. Poultry is also cooked by dry or moist heat, depending upon its tenderness.

Meat, poultry, and fish must be refrigerated or frozen to keep them fresh and safe to eat. These foods are good sources of protein.

Vegetables are good sources of vitamins A and C and fiber, and they're low in calories. Good quality vegetables are fresh and crisp. Vegetables can be cooked or eaten raw. Vegetables should be cooked properly to keep their color and their nutrients.

What Have You Learned?

1. Explain why some meat is more tender than other meat.
2. What is the difference between moist-heat cooking and dry-heat cooking?
3. How should meat, poultry, and fish be stored? Why?
4. How do you cook vegetables to keep their color and nutrients?
5. A dinner menu is usually planned around meat, poultry, or fish. What does this mean? Give some examples.
6. Give the right order for clearing the table.

Things to Do

1. Look at the list of "All the Things You Can Do With Ground Beef!" on page 210. Then check through cookbooks. Think of three cooking ideas to add to the chart.
2. Do a grocery store survey. Make a list of all the vegetables which are new to you.
3. Practice serving a meal to a classmate. Practice clearing the table while the classmate is seated.
4. Practice holding a cup of liquid and placing it on a table without spilling it.

ENTERTAINING FRIENDS

buffet style	food put on the table in serving dishes so guests can serve themselves, then carry their food someplace else to eat
entertaining	having a party or inviting someone home
flour	to cover lightly with flour
frosting	cake topping
host	boy or man who entertains guests
hostess	girl or woman who entertains guests
invitation	asking someone to come as a guest
party mix	mixture of nuts, seeds, and other dry snack foods
punch	beverage made by mixing several beverages
reception	a type of party, usually given to welcome someone
refreshments	food and beverages served at a party
RSVP	to let the host or hostess know whether you will attend
sherbet	frozen dessert similar to ice cream

After reading this chapter, you should be able to:

- *write a party invitation.*
- *list five things a good host or hostess must do.*
- *plan a party menu.*
- *list five nutritious party foods.*
- *plan a class party.*

D o you enjoy visiting a friend after school? Do you like to go to parties? Inviting people to your home is an offer of friendship. Having a party is called *entertaining.* So is asking friends over to your home after school. Food is often a major part of entertaining. Both teenagers and adults like to eat when they get together. The important thing is to serve something guests like and to serve it attractively.

Food is often a major part of entertaining—whether for children, teenagers, or adults.

Having a Few Friends Over

When you entertain, it's a fun time to experiment with food. Sometimes you may think, "There's nothing special to eat!" You'd be surprised. There are probably many good snacks in your kitchen.

Pretend you are going to have some friends over. Think of easy ways to make these foods special for them: crackers and cheese, cookies and milk, bread and peanut butter, fresh fruit, ice cream and cookies. You might think of these ideas to make the snacks special:

- Arrange the food attractively on a plate.
- Use colorful napkins.
- Cut peanut butter sandwiches into interesting shapes.
- Pour milk into glasses. Add a straw for fun. Don't just put the carton on the table. A milk container isn't attractive on the table.

These are simple ideas. But they do make a difference.

Giving a Party

Let's have a party! Maybe you have a special event to celebrate, such as winning a basketball game or celebrating a birthday. If not, make up a reason. Have a dance marathon or a "come as your favorite movie star" party.

Before you make too many plans, check with your family. An adult should be home when you entertain. A party takes a lot of planning. It takes a lot of work, too. For practice, your class might entertain the faculty or your parents.

Invitations to a Party

If you want guests, you must invite them. First, decide how many people you can invite. Then call them on the phone, ask them when you're with them, or send a written invitation. An *invitation* is asking someone to come as a guest. When you invite guests, you must tell them:

- where the party will be
- the day and time
- the kind of party. For example, is it a slumber party or a birthday party?
- if you want them to RSVP. To *RSVP* is to let the host or hostess know you will attend.

It's always nice to let your guests know who else is coming to the party. Sometimes friends like to come to a party together.

A written invitation must tell the kind of party, where it will be and when. RSVP means you should let the host or hostess know if you will attend. "Please reply" means the same thing.

Party Food and Fun

Food is part of party fun. Decide what to serve for refreshments. *Refreshments* are the foods and beverages served at a party. Remember, food doesn't have to be fancy. You might plan food that is:

- easy to prepare
- easy to serve
- pleasing to guests

At a party, food is often served buffet style. *Buffet style* is putting the food on the table in serving dishes. Guests help themselves, then they carry their food somewhere else to eat. No places are set at a buffet table.

Here's another way to serve. Put the food on plates, then take it to guests. Just be sure the food and plate is easy to carry! Or put plates of food around the room.

Your party may be more successful if you plan something fun to do. Of course, entertaining at home is different from entertaining at school. You can really do more at home. Play records or tapes. Plan some games like charades or Twenty Questions.

If it's a special time of year, plan a theme party. For example, a Halloween party is a theme party. Have a costume contest or bob for apples. Decorate to make the party more interesting.

Buffet style is an easy way to serve a large number of people at a party.

A good host or hostess makes everyone at a party feel comfortable—even those who don't know anyone else. One thing to do is to introduce them to the other guests.

Being a Good Host or Hostess

When a girl or woman entertains, she's a *hostess*. When a boy or man entertains, he's a *host*. Learning to be a good host or hostess helps you and your guests enjoy the party. What does a host or hostess do? A good host or hostess:

- has the room neat, clean, and ready for a party.
- plans enough seating space so everyone is comfortable.
- has food and beverages ready to serve.
- greets people at the door.
- makes everyone feel comfortable and welcome.
- introduces people who haven't met.
- plans time well and doesn't spend too much time away from guests.
- spends time with every guest, not just a few.
- serves refreshments early enough so people can enjoy eating before they have to go home.
- makes sure everything is picked up after the party.

Polite guests thank the host or hostess when leaving a party.

Being a Good Guest

Being a good guest is as important as being a good host or hostess. People want to entertain friends who are thoughtful. Do you want to be invited to parties? Then be a good guest by:

- letting the host or hostess know if you can accept the invitation.
- arriving on time.
- helping the host or hostess if asked.
- acting in a way that won't embarrass the host or hostess.
- not making a mess.
- tasting the refreshments, even if you don't think you'll like what's served.
- not staying too long.
- thanking the host or hostess.

Party Foods

What's on the menu? You can serve almost anything for a party. It just needs to look good and taste good.

For special holidays, there are some foods that just seem right. Thanksgiving, for example, is a time when many serve a turkey dinner to guests. For the Fourth of July, hot dogs and hamburgers are good cooked over the grill.

Think about your family holidays. What do you like to serve?

Some foods like turkey are associated with particular holidays. Turkey is a symbol of the Thanksgiving holiday.

Dry Snacks

Dry, crunchy snacks are party favorites. Popcorn, chips, and pretzels are popular. You have other choices, too. Serve peanuts, or even sunflower seeds.

Peanuts and sunflower seeds are nutritious choices. Both are high in protein. What other foods are high in protein? You're right if you said "meat," "poultry," or "fish." Nuts and seeds belong in the Meat, Poultry, Fish, and Beans Group.

You can use these foods to make your own party mix. A *party mix* is a mixture of nuts, seeds, and other dry snack foods, such as coconut and chopped, dried fruit. You can buy these snacks in the store, but it's more fun and often cheaper to mix them yourself.

Serve dry snacks in bowls. You might have several bowls around the room. Then your guests can easily help themselves.

Fruit kabobs—small pieces of fruit on a tooth pick or small skewer make attractive and nutritious party foods.

Vegetable and Fruit Snacks

Raw vegetables and fruit are crunchy snacks, too. What's more, they're low in calories. What nutrients are in vegetables and fruit? A plate of fresh vegetables or fruit is pretty to look at.

One way of making an attractive fruit snack is to cut fruit into small pieces. Thread two or three pieces of fruit on a toothpick. A grape, an apple slice, and an orange section are good. Another way is to cut raw vegetables into large pieces. Have several kinds: sliced cucumbers, celery sticks, broccoli flowerettes, sliced carrots, and whole mushrooms. Toss them together in a bowl or arrange them neatly on a platter. Serve with a favorite dip.

Hearty Snacks

Almost everyone loves pizza. Think of all the ingredients in your favorite pizza. Did you say "sausage," "cheese," "mushrooms," or "green peppers"? These foods are all nutritious. Pizza is made on a bread crust. The sauce is made with tomatoes. Pizza belongs in all four main food groups!

Pizza is easy to make for a party. You can make it from scratch. Or buy prepared pizza in the store and bake it according to the package directions.

Tacos are good for parties, too. They are especially fun if the party has a Mexican theme. Tacos are a Mexican food.

Like pizza, tacos are nutritious. The taco shell belongs in the Bread and Cereal Group. You fill the taco with cooked meat, lettuce, tomatoes, and cheese. What food groups do these foods belong in?

Party Desserts

Some parties are dessert parties. Earlier, you learned that desserts are served at the end of a meal. You can have dessert as the main party food, too.

What about an ice cream party? Serve bowls of ice cream to everyone. Nuts, chopped fruit, and coconut taste good as toppings. Put each topping in a separate bowl. Let your guests put on their own toppings.

Cake Making   Birthdays and cakes seem to go together. Cakes are nice to make for other parties, too. Decorate cakes to make them special.

Cakes are made from flour, eggs, sugar, a liquid, and a few other ingredients. The ingredients are mixed into a batter. Remember that a batter is a thin mixture of flour, liquid, and other ingredients. And then they're baked until they're done.

How do you make a cake? You must follow the directions in the recipe carefully. Cake mixes make cake making easy. They are convenience foods that come in many different flavors and varieties. Some contain fat, such as butter and oil. Chocolate cake is an example—others such as angel food cakes, contain no fat. Cakes can be made in many shapes.

- Make a sheet cake in a baking pan.
- Make a layer cake. Divide the batter into two smaller pans. Be sure you have an equal amount in each pan. Your teacher can show you how.
- Make cupcakes or small cakes in muffin tins. Again, ask your teacher to show you how.

Frosting is a cake topping. Some cakes are best with a frosting. Others are good without it. You can make frosting or buy canned frosting for convenience.

BAKING A CAKE FROM A MIX

1 Read the directions on the mix. Set the oven to the desired temperature so it will preheat while you are preparing the mix and the pans. Put shortening on a paper towel or wax paper. Then spread it lightly on the bottom and sides of the cake pan.

2 Flour the cake pans. To *flour* is to cover lightly with flour. Sprinkle a spoonful of flour into each pan. Then shake the pan. The flour will cover the shortening. Throw away any extra flour.

3 Pour the mix into a bowl. Add the other ingredients. Blend the ingredients with an electric mixer.

4 Pour the batter into the pans and spread it evenly to the sides of the pan.

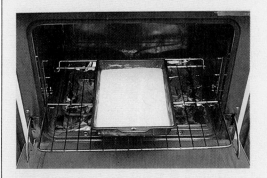

5 Bake your cake in the center of the oven. Follow the directions for baking time.

6 Test to be sure the cake is done. Put a toothpick into the cake's center. It should come out clean. Ask your teacher to show you.

7 When the cake is done, let it cool in the pan. Put the pan on the cooling rack.

8 Frost the cake. Put frosting in the center, then spread it to the edges. For convenience, use frosting in a can.

Party Beverages

What will you serve to drink? Punch? Fruit juice? Soft drinks?

Soft drinks are fun foods. You might enjoy them for a party. But they aren't nutritious. Some have calories from carbohydrate but no other nutrients. Low-calorie soft drinks are really flavored water.

Why not drink something that tastes even better? A combination of fruit juices tastes good, and it's good for you, too. Add ice cream to the drink for extra flavor and nutrients.

Punch—A Party Drink *Punch* is an easy beverage for a crowd. Some punches are cold, while others are hot. Punch is actually made of several different beverages. Pour it into a big bowl and let guests serve themselves, using a ladle to pour the punch into glasses or cups.

These are three punch ideas:

- Serve hot cider. Float orange slices in the cider.
- Combine cold pineapple juice, lemon-lime soft drinks, and lime sherbet. *Sherbet* is similar to ice cream, but the ingredients are slightly different.
- Combine cold milk and chocolate syrup. Blend in scoops of mint ice cream.

Let's Have a Class Party!

Now you know about parties. Practice by giving a party in class. What kind of party could you have? Who might you invite? Teachers from your school might like to come. Or invite your parents or another class.

You might have a party with a Mexican theme. Mexican food is very popular and very tasty. Earlier, you learned that Mexican food is ethnic food. For a Mexican-style party, you might make tacos and fruit punch, learn to dance the Mexican Hat Dance or ask a Spanish class to help decorate.

A *reception* is a quieter party. It's a nice welcome for new students to your school or for parents to see your home economics class. At a reception you might:

- serve cake, cookies, or a plate of fresh fruit. For beverages, serve punch. Remember that coffee and tea are nice for adults.
- set the table with a pretty centerpiece.
- make name tags so it's easy to introduce guests.

What other good ideas do you have?

CHAPTER REVIEW

Summary

Food is often part of entertaining. Food served to friends can be simple, but it should still look attractive.

A party usually takes quite a bit of planning. The host or hostess invites guests, plans food and any entertainment, and prepares the food. The person giving the party also knows how to be a good host or hostess. Being a good guest is important, too.

Any food can be a party food. Dry snacks, raw vegetables, and fresh fruit are all nice party foods. Hearty snacks, such as pizza and tacos, are good when guests have big appetites. Party desserts such as cake, cookies, and ice cream are often served, too. Punch is a party beverage.

What Have You Learned?

1. What should you include in your invitation?
2. Name six things a good host or hostess does at a party?
3. Name three ways you can be a good guest.
4. What simple snacks could you serve to a friend today?
5. Explain why nuts, seeds, and some beans are in the Meat, Poultry, Fish, and Beans Group.
6. Explain why pizza and tacos are nutritious snacks.
7. How could you serve raw vegetables and fruit at a party?
8. Why is punch nice to serve for guests?

Things to Do

1. Think of the next time you want to have friends over. For practice, write an invitation. Be sure you list all the important information.
2. Plan a special party for a friend or someone in your family. Choose a theme, a menu, and party entertainment.
3. Look for easy party snacks in cookbooks. Share three ideas with the class.
4. Cakes can be decorated in many different ways. Look in magazines. Describe five different ways to decorate a cake.

SHOPPING FOR FOOD

comparison shopping	comparing items to get the best buy for your money
consumer	person who buys and uses certain items, such as food
coupon	a certificate that offers cents off the price of certain foods
impulse buying	buying something you didn't plan to
nutrient label	information on a food label that tells what nutrients the food contains and the amount of each nutrient one serving will provide
rain check	a certificate that lets you buy a food at the sale price in the future if the store runs out of the item during the sale
unit price	price of a food per pound, ounce, or quart

After reading this chapter, you should be able to:

- *make a shopping list.*
- *list the reasons for shopping in a supermarket, specialty store, and convenience store.*
- *identify five ways to stretch your food dollar.*
- *read a food label.*
- *compare fresh, frozen, and canned foods.*

G ood cooks know how to prepare food well. They also know how to shop wisely for food. They get their money's worth at the store. Buying food is like buying clothes. Do you know why? When you buy either food or clothes, you should:

- look at the price to decide if you can afford it.
- look to see if the quality is good.
- decide if it's what you need.
- compare prices at other stores to see if you can find better quality for the same price or less.

Getting Ready to Shop

A trip to buy groceries, or food supplies, starts at home. A good shopper saves time and money by deciding what to buy before entering the store.

Planning Meals

Wise shopping starts with carefully planned menus. Remember the guidelines for menu planning:

- Consider your food budget.
- Consider the season of the year. Some foods, such as strawberries and watermelon, aren't available all year. Foods usually cost less when they are in season.
- Consider how much time you have to prepare food. When time is short, convenience foods are useful.
- Include foods you have on hand, such as leftovers.
- Consider who is eating, their likes, dislikes, and schedules.
- Plan nutritious, appealing meals. Use the four main food groups!

Smart shopping is an important part of being a good cook.

Preparing a Shopping List

A shopping list helps you save both time and money. Review the menu, then list exactly what foods you need. You'll avoid unnecessary purchases and extra trips to the grocery store.

This is how to make and use a shopping list:

- Keep your list handy. Some people keep it on the refrigerator door with a magnet. Write down foods, such as flour or seasonings, as they get low.
- Complete the list after you plan your meals and snacks. Write down the ingredients from the menu and the specific recipes.
- Check the kitchen to see what's on hand. Then cross off the foods you already have.
- List foods as they are grouped in the store. For example, list each type of food together—fresh fruits and vegetables; fresh meat, fish, and poultry; canned and dry foods; frozen foods; dairy foods; and non-food items.
- When you shop, check off each item as you put it in your cart.

Making a list ahead of time will help you avoid unnecessary purchases and extra trips to the store. Listing the foods as they're grouped in the store will save you time in the store.

Before shopping, check to see what supplies you already have and cross them off your list.

Impulse buying can be avoided if we eat before we shop—and buy only what's on our list.

Avoiding Impulse Buying

Planned shopping can help you avoid impulse buying. *Impulse buying* is buying something you didn't plan to buy because it looks or smells good, because it's new, or because "you just felt like it."

Store managers want people to buy on impulse. They display food in ways that will catch your eye. For example, some items are near the check-out line. It's easy to reach for these things while you wait in line. They also encourage you to buy by offering a free sample to taste. These things can cause you to spend money you haven't planned to spend.

You can avoid impulse buying in these ways:

- Prepare a shopping list, and buy only what's on it.
- Don't go to the store hungry. Hungry shoppers tend to buy more.
- Buy enough so you don't need to shop too often. The more often you go to the store, the more you'll be likely to buy.

Where to Shop

Many types of stores sell food. How do you know where to shop? The store that's best for you:

- has the quality and variety of foods you need.
- sells fresh-looking produce, meat, poultry, and fish.
- keeps refrigerated foods cold.
- is clean and well arranged.
- keeps the shelves full.
- is priced fairly.
- provides good service.
- is easy to get to.

Different types of food stores meet different needs. Some are less expensive, some carry specific foods, and some are close by and quick.

Supermarkets

Supermarkets are big food stores with thousands of items to choose from. Some sell already cooked foods to take out. Others have drug stores, flower shops, or small restaurants. Many offer special services such as check cashing or delivery service.

If you shop carefully, supermarkets can have the best prices with the widest selection.

Specialty Stores

Smaller stores might specialize in one type of food. Bakeries and ethnic food stores are specialty stores. A store which sells mainly ingredients for making foreign foods is an ethnic food store. For example, an Asian food store is an ethnic food store.

Specialty stores often carry foods you can't find elsewhere. Sometimes the foods they sell are more expensive, but not always.

Convenience Stores

Convenience stores are just what their name says—convenient, or handy. They sell just the basic foods without much choice. And they're usually open when other stores are closed. Many stay open 24 hours a day.

In convenience stores, food usually costs more. You pay extra for the convenience of all-night service and a handy location.

Getting Your Money's Worth

People spend money on many things. Housing, clothes, a car, and entertainment are all examples of things people spend their money on. Food is another major item in the household budget. By shopping carefully, you can get the most for the money you have to spend on food.

Comparison Shopping

Comparison shopping is one way to get the most for your food dollar. *Comparison shopping* involves comparing the cost, nutrients, ingredients, and freshness of similar foods in order to choose the best food for the most reasonable price.

This teenager is comparing the cost and nutrients of two beverages.

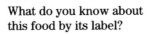

What do you know about this food by its label?

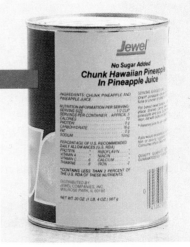

Food Labels Have you looked carefully at a food label? If so, you know that a food label is full of information for comparison shopping. Food labels can tell you about the food, its ingredients, the nutrients, and ways to prepare it.

A label tells you about the food in the package. Every label must give this information:

- kind of food
- brand name
- company that made or packaged it
- address of the company
- amount by weight or volume
- the food's form

WHAT'S ON A NUTRIENT LABEL?

A nutritional label must include:

- serving size
- number of servings in the package
- calories in one serving
- amount of carbohydrate, fat, and protein in one serving
- percentage of the recommended daily amounts of several nutrients in one serving

The form of the food is the way it's sold, such as sliced, packed in water, or made into juice. Buy the kind that's best for your intended use. You don't need to buy whole, canned tomatoes for spaghetti sauce. Buy crushed tomatoes instead since they're cheaper.

Many food labels also give nutritional information. The *nutrient label* tells what nutrients the food contains, and the amount of each nutrient one serving will provide.

By law, most food labels must list the ingredients, too. The ingredients are listed in order by weight. The ingredient that is present in the greatest amount is listed first and the ingredient that is used least is listed last. The ingredient list can help you compare foods like beef stew. The label which lists beef first probably has more beef than the one that lists beef third.

Unit Pricing How much does a food item cost? Many supermarkets show the price on the shelf just below the food. This shelf label gives the package price along with the unit price.

The *unit price* is the cost per pound, ounce, or maybe quart. With this information, you can compare several different brands and container sizes to see which is cheapest per unit.

Often the largest size is the least expensive. You can tell by reading the unit price labels. Sometimes the biggest isn't the best buy. Don't buy the big size if kitchen space is limited or if it'll spoil before you can use it all.

Generic products have no brand name, they have less information on the label and they are usually the least expensive.

Newspaper ads and coupons can help you save money when you shop for food.

Food Advertisements

Food advertisements help people save money. They tell what foods have been reduced in price or put "on sale." Most supermarkets offer weekly "specials" to get business. "Specials" are foods sold at reduced prices.

Newspapers advertise stores' food "specials" weekly. Most stores display these advertisements by the door. They're also printed in community newspapers.

Coupons

Coupons can save money, too. *Coupons* offer cents off the price of certain foods. Give the cashier your coupons before the order is added up. The coupons' values are subtracted from your bill. "Double-coupon days" offer even more savings. Stores may double the coupon value for a short time.

Coupons are printed in magazine and newspaper advertisements, and on package labels. Sometimes they come in the mail. Remember that coupons only offer savings if you need what you buy.

Convenience Foods

Convenience foods may save you time but not money. They usually cost more because you pay for the food plus the preparation. Even so, it sometimes makes sense to buy convenience foods:

- Saving time might be more important than saving money. For example, it's fast to heat canned soup.
- Having convenience foods on the shelf or in the freezer is good for emergencies. You have food on hand for an unexpected guest or a time when you can't cook.
- Convenience foods can be stored longer than most fresh foods. Then you need to shop less often. For example, frozen orange juice keeps longer than fresh oranges.
- Sometimes convenience foods are cheaper than cooking yourself. For example, a TV dinner which serves one or two people might be cheaper than buying all the ingredients it would take to prepare the same meal.
- Some foods, such as French croissants, are hard to make. Croissants are crescent-shaped, flaky rolls. With convenience foods, you can still have these hard-to-make foods.

Storing What You Purchase

Once shopping is done, take food home right away. If you stop for errands, some foods may lose their quality. For example, ice cream will melt, lettuce can wilt, and meat and milk which become too warm will start to spoil.

At home put refrigerated items into the refrigerator immediately and frozen items into the freezer. Then, put away the other items.

Groceries should be taken home and put away right after purchasing so they won't spoil.

254

Consumer Rights

Consumers have certain rights when they shop. A *consumer* is a person who buys and uses items such as food.

Damaged Products

Sometimes products are already damaged or spoiled when they're sold. Consumers have the right to return the item and get their money back. If this happens, these are your responsibilities as a consumer:

- Keep the package as it was when you bought it. Certainly don't eat any food from a package you are planning to return.
- Return the package with the receipt. The receipt is the cash register slip which acts as a record of your purchase.
- Bring it back as soon as possible.

Rain Checks

What happens when the store runs out of a food on a special sale? Many stores give rain checks. A *rain check* lets you buy the food later at the lower price, even if it's no longer on sale.

Rain checks are usually given out at the customer service desk. You need to ask for them. Usually rain checks must be used within a few weeks.

Incorrect Price

The grocery bill is added up at the check-out counter. Most cash registers display the price of each item you buy. It's a good idea for you to know the prices and to watch as your bill is added up. You can also check the receipt.

If you were incorrectly charged, point it out politely to the cashier. Your bill will be fixed if there was a mistake.

Incorrect Change

Although it doesn't happen often, cashiers can make mistakes when they handle money. Always count your change before you leave the checkout line. If the cashier made an error, point it out politely. It will usually be handled immediately by the cashier.

Comparing Fresh, Frozen, and Canned Foods

Which is the best buy—fresh, frozen, or canned foods? It all depends. By comparing them in the store and in the kitchen, you can decide which one is best for you.

As a laboratory activity, compare foods in three forms: fresh, frozen, and canned. You might compare foods such as green beans, peas, corn, carrots, peaches, and orange juice in each of the three forms. As you compare, write your observations on paper. These are things to look for:

- **Price.** Decide what size one serving of each food is. Then determine the price per serving of each food.
- **Packaging.** How is the food packaged?
- **Storage.** Where is the food stored? How long can it be safely stored?
- **Preparation.** What do you have to do before the food can be eaten? For example, does it have to be mixed with other ingredients before you can eat or drink it? Does the package give directions? How long will it take to prepare?
- **Appearance.** How does the food look when it's ready to eat? What are the color and shape like?
- **Texture.** How does the food feel in your mouth?
- **Taste.** How does the food taste?

After you finish your comparison, decide how this food is best used in a meal or snack. What conclusions can you draw from your observations?

Good consumers compare foods in many ways. They want to get the best buy for the money they spend on food. You can be a good consumer, too.

Most foods come in different forms. To determine which is best for you compare the price, the packaging, the storage, the preparation time, the appearance, the texture, and the taste of fresh, frozen and canned.

CHAPTER REVIEW

Summary

Wise shoppers plan ahead. Planning menus and preparing a shopping list are two ways to avoid impulse shopping. Choosing the right store also saves time and money. Supermarkets, specialty stores, and convenience stores are three different places to buy food. Supermarkets are usually cheapest, but convenience stores are handy.

Consumers must shop carefully to get the best buy. To get the most for their money, consumers can comparison shop, use coupons, read food advertisements, and use convenience foods carefully.

What Have You Learned?

1. Why is a shopping list important?
2. What are three ways you might avoid impulse shopping?
3. What are the advantages and disadvantages of shopping in a supermarket? Specialty store? Convenience store?
4. What information might you find on a food label?
5. How can you use the nutrient label to compare foods?
6. What are five ways you can save money on food shopping?
7. Why should foods be taken home as soon as they are purchased?
8. What should you do if a cereal box you bought was damaged in the store?

Things to Do

1. Bring the food ads from several newspapers to class. Compare the prices of five foods to see who has the best buy.
2. Compare the prices of four food items in a supermarket, a convenience store, and, if possible, a specialty store. Use unit prices if you can. Report your findings to the class.
3. Visit a supermarket to find out where different foods are found.
4. Make a store map to show these departments: produce (fresh fruits and vegetables), meat, baking ingredients, canned fruits and vegetables, frozen foods, dairy products, and others. Show where the checkout counter is.

EATING OUT

a la carte	when each food is ordered separately on the menu
course	all the foods that are served at one time
entree	main course
fast foods	foods prepared and served fast in a restaurant
gourmet restaurants	fancy restaurants which offer elaborately prepared meals
reservation	place held for you, generally in a restaurant
tip	payment for service

After reading this chapter, you should be able to:

- *compare food and service in a fast-food restaurant, family restaurant, and cafeteria.*
- *describe the food served in three ethnic restaurants.*
- *order from a menu.*
- *explain when and how much to tip in a restaurant.*
- *list five rules for proper restaurant manners.*

A t least one-third of all meals are eaten away from home. Why is this so? We live very busy lives. We are away from home at school or work for many hours of a day. Eating out may be more convenient than going home to eat or carrying food with us. We also like to eat in restaurants for relaxation. And it is also fun to try new foods.

Eating Away from Home

Where do you go when you eat out? Fast-food restaurants, family restaurants, cafeterias, fancy restaurants, ethnic restaurants, even your school cafeteria are among the choices you have. Your choice will depend on where you are, how much money you have, and what kind of food you want to eat.

Fast food restaurants are a popular choice for people eating away from home.

School Cafeteria

Eating in the school cafeteria is eating out. The school lunch is planned to be a nutritious meal. By law, it must have five different foods representing the food groups.

In most schools, you can take three, four, or five of the foods served. But you must pay the same price no matter how many you take.

School lunch doesn't cost much because the government helps pay for the meals. There are also free or reduced lunch prices for students who can't afford the full price. Usually, a school lunch costs less than a lunch you carry from home.

Besides the school lunch, some schools have an *a la carte* line. There you buy each food separately. From an a la carte line, meals cost more because the government doesn't help pay for these foods. In some places, you can eat breakfast at school, too.

If you eat in the school cafeteria, do be thoughtful of others. Clean up your tray and waste paper, and leave your seat at the table neat when you leave.

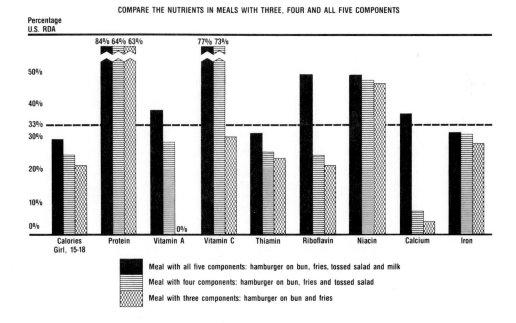

COMPARE THE NUTRIENTS IN MEALS WITH THREE, FOUR AND ALL FIVE COMPONENTS

Meal with all five components: hamburger on bun, fries, tossed salad and milk

Meal with four components: hamburger on bun, fries and tossed salad

Meal with three components: hamburger on bun and fries

Fast-Food Restaurants

Fast-food restaurants are just what their name says—fast. Both the preparation and the service are quick. These restaurants usually provide clean surroundings and consistent food quality.

In a fast-food restaurant, the menu is posted on the wall where you order. You pay at the time you order. The menu in a fast-food restaurant is more limited than in other types of restaurants. For this reason, you can be served faster.

Today, there are many different fast-food restaurants to choose from. For example, you can have seafood, hamburgers, Mexican food, salad bars, stuffed potatoes, pizza, and Greek sandwiches all from different types of fast-food restaurants.

A meal in a fast-food restaurant can be very nutritious. A hamburger with lettuce and tomato, fries, and milk has foods from the four main food groups. Salad bars offer a variety of vegetables and fruit. If you are watching calories, know that a quarter-pound hamburger, fries, and a shake are a high-calorie combination.

Cafeterias are another place where food service is fast. You are served from steam tables as you walk through the line. You pay at the end of the line.

Family Restaurants

Family restaurants are usually more leisurely than fast-food restaurants. Diners and coffee shops are examples of family restaurants. In a family restaurant, you order from a menu at the table. Usually you have more choices than in a fast-food restaurant, and the food is brought to you.

Family restaurants usually cost a little more than fast-food restaurants. That's partly because they offer more service.

There are many choices available in fast food restaurants in addition to the popular hamburger, fries, and cola.

© 1986 TACO BELL CORP.

Family restaurants usually provide you with more choices than fast food restaurants.

Gourmet restaurants offer elegant food, service, and surroundings. These restaurants usually cost more than family restaurants.

Fancy Restaurants

A fancy restaurant offers elaborate food and service. Fancy restaurants are often called gourmet restaurants. You usually need a reservation to eat there. A *reservation* means that you called ahead and a place has been held for you.

At a gourmet restaurant, the food takes a lot of time and care to prepare and is cooked in very precise methods. Each dish may be prepared just for you. This type of restaurant usually has more people to wait on you, too.

At gourmet restaurants, tablecloths and cloth napkins are usually used. Often, there are flowers on the table. Decorations, such as crystal chandeliers, plants, and soft lights, make the dining room special. You pay more for the attractive surroundings and the special foods.

Eating in a gourmet restaurant may take a couple of hours. This is a place to eat on very special occasions.

Ethnic Restaurants

Many restaurants serve food with a foreign flavor. Ethnic foods are foods which are associated with people from another culture, usually another country.

In the United States, there are many different ethnic restaurants. That's partly because people from all over the world have come to live here. They brought their foods and recipes with them.

Ethnic restaurants feature special recipes of the country. Often, these specialties are listed on the menu in the native language. If you eat at an ethnic restaurant, you may ask the waiter or waitress to explain the menu terms.

Italian Restaurants Many people order pizza and spaghetti in an Italian restaurant. But Italian restaurants serve many other foods.

Italian restaurants are known for pasta. Remember, noodles are one kind of pasta. Pasta actually comes in over 300 different shapes! An Italian restaurant combines pasta with meat, seafood, vegetables, cheese, and different sauces to make many different dishes. Spaghetti, lasagna, and fettucini are three examples.

Dinner in an Italian restaurant might start with an appetizer called antipasto. This might be followed by soup or pasta. The main course would be meat or fish with vegetables, and Italian bread. Salad may come next, and last, a dessert of cheese and fruit.

Mexican Restaurants Mexican restaurants may serve fast-food style or family style. Two advantages of Mexican foods are their low cost and good nutrition.

What we now call Mexican food had its start with the Aztec Indians who lived in Mexico hundreds of years ago. When Spanish settlers came, they brought their own food customs with them. Over the years, the customs of the two cultures mixed and became today's Mexican food.

Corn, rice, beans, tomatoes, and chili peppers are important ingredients in Mexican dishes. Tortillas are part of many Mexican dishes. Tortillas are flat pancakes made of corn or wheat. Sometimes they're eaten plain. They may also be used to make tacos, enchiladas, burritos, tostadas, and chimichangas. Rice and refried beans are usually served with these foods.

In the United States, most foods served in Mexican restaurants are really a combination of Texas and Mexican, or Tex-Mex foods.

Ethnic restaurants offer foods common to a particular country or culture.

Italian

Chinese

Mexican

Japanese

Chinese Restaurants   Chinese restaurants are very popular in the United States. Although most restaurants serve chop suey and chow mein, these foods did not start in China. Chinese foods are typically made with many vegetables and small amounts of lean meat, poultry, or fish. The recipes are high in nutrients and low in fat and calories. So Chinese food is very healthful.

Stir-frying is one important method of cooking Chinese foods. Do you remember how to stir-fry vegetables? Meat and vegetables are sliced thin, then cooked quickly in a little oil. They stay crisp and colorful. Having food in small pieces makes it easy to eat with chopsticks instead of a knife and fork. In a Chinese restaurant, your meal will be served with a bowl of rice. Tea is served in small cups without handles. Fruit or fortune cookies are common desserts.

Japanese Restaurants   Besides Chinese, other Oriental restaurants are popular. Japanese restaurants are one example. Japanese meals have many different dishes. The foods are light, and the portions are small, but they are very nutritious.

Some of the cooking methods are similar to the Chinese. Japanese foods are often cut into small pieces and stir-fried. Many Japanese restaurants in the United States cook on a hibachi. A hibachi is a grill for stir-frying built into the middle of the table.

These ingredients are important in Japanese cooking: fish, seaweed, soybeans, and rice. Like many Asian meals, rice is served with the meal.

In Japanese cooking, art is very important. The color, shape, and arrangement of food is carefully planned.

Other Ethnic Restaurants.   There are many other kinds of ethnic restaurants, especially in big cities. Many French restaurants serve gourmet food. German restaurants often serve pork dishes with sauerkraut and dumplings. Greek restaurants might serve lamb, salads, or sandwiches in pita, or pocket bread. Are there any other kinds of ethnic restaurants in your town? You might find it interesting to find out. Better yet, learn about new foods by going there to eat.

Restaurant Manners

When you eat away from home, there are some things you need to know. You should know how to order from a menu, how to pay the bill, and how to leave a tip. You also need to be thoughtful of others in the restaurant.

Ordering from a Menu

Except for fast-food restaurants and cafeterias, you order from a printed menu. The menu is given to you by a waiter or waitress when you sit at the table. The menu lists the foods you can order along with the price for each food.

Most foods on menus are arranged by courses. A *course* includes all the foods served at one time. These are the courses on many menus: appetizers, soups, salads, entrees, vegetables, and desserts. Remember that an appetizer is the first course of a meal. *Entrees* are foods served as the main dish.

After the entrees on a menu, there may be a note explaining what is included. For example, it might say, "Choice of potato or vegetable, rolls, and beverage included." If there is no note, only the main dish is served for the price stated. On an a la carte menu, you must order each food separately. If you are ordering a complete meal this is a more expensive way to order, but your choices are greater.

Menus vary according to the type of restaurant. Some are very elaborate, others are short— sometimes written on a chalk board. In fast food restaurants the menu is usually on the wall behind the counter.

The menu may have words that are new to you. Menu items might be given in a language other than English. If you don't know what a food is, politely ask the waiter or waitress.

When you are ready to order, tell the waiter or waitress what you want. Don't keep him or her waiting too long.

WORDS ON ETHNIC MENUS

Italian

antipasto (an tee PAHS toh)—appetizer salad of meat, vegetables, and cheese

fettucini (feh too CHEE nee)—thin noodles tossed with cream and Parmesan cheese

lasagna (lah SAH nyah)—wide noodles layered with ricotta cheese, meat, and tomato sauce

marinara (MAIR ih NAIR ah)—spicy tomato sauce without meat

minestrone (mih nih STROH nee)—thick vegetable soup

parmigiana (par mih gih AH nah)—made with Parmesan cheese

spumoni (spoo MOH nee)—ice cream made with fruit and nuts

Mexican

burrito (bur REE to)—tortilla wrapped around meat or bean filling

enchilada (en chih LAH dah)—tortillas filled with meat or chicken and vegetables, then baked

taco (TAH coh)—fried tortilla folded and filled with meat, tomatoes, cheese, and lettuce

tortilla (tor TEE yah)—flat bread made from cornmeal or wheat flour

tostada (tohs TAH dah)—tortilla fried and topped with meat, tomatoes, cheese, and lettuce

Chinese

chop suey (chop SOO ee)—meat and vegetables served over rice

chow mein (chow mayn)—meat and vegetables served over fried noodles

egg foo yung (eg foo yung)—eggs made like an omelet

egg rolls—thin pancake filled with egg, chopped vegetables and meat, poultry, or fish, then fried

fried rice—rice mixed with meat, poultry, fish, eggs, vegetables, and seasonings

won tons (won tonz)—dumplings, often fried

Japanese

sukiyaki (soo kee YAK kee)—beef and vegetables stir-fried at the table

tempura (tem PUR ah)—meat, poultry, fish, or vegetables dipped in batter, then fried

teriyaki (tair ee YAH kee)—slices of meat, poultry, or seafood cooked with a special sauce

Considering Others

Good manners are important, even at a fast-food restaurant. These are some rules to follow:

- Speak softly in a restaurant. Only the people at your table should hear your conversation.
- If you want to talk to someone at another table, excuse yourself from your own table. Then go to the person you wish to talk with.
- If someone else is paying the bill, order thoughtfully. Don't order the most costly food.
- Wait until everyone is served before you start eating.
- If a food isn't prepared right, ask the waiter or waitress to correct this. Don't make a fuss, however. Most restaurants want to serve well-prepared food.
- In a fast-food restaurant and some cafeterias, it is necessary to clean up the table after you eat. Throw away the paper and stack the tray.

Paying the Bill and Tipping

When you finish eating, the waiter or waitress will bring you the bill. Check the bill to make sure it's correct.

In some restaurants, you pay the cashier as you leave. In other restaurants, you pay the waiter or waitress. It's polite to tell the waiter or waitress ahead if each person plans to pay separately. That makes it easier to figure the bill. Decide before you enter the restaurant who is paying the bill and how it will be divided.

You also leave a tip on the table for the waiter or waitress. A *tip* is what you pay for service. The tip is extra—it's usually not in your bill. If the tip is in the bill, you don't have to pay it twice.

If you think the service was good, your tip should be between 15 and 20 percent of the bill. If the service could be better, you can pay less. If your bill was very small, leave at least fifteen cents per person.

Remember that the tip is usually the biggest part of a waiter's or waitress's pay. It's not thoughtful to leave without tipping unless the service was bad. If you had that job, you would want good tips. You don't need to tip in a cafeteria or fast-food restaurant. That's because there are no waiters or waitresses to serve you.

Don't forget to leave a tip for the service.

Some restaurants, or perhaps your school cafeteria, have taco bars. Here you make your own tacos. You could make your own taco bar at home.

Making Tacos

Tacos are a favorite restaurant food. Schools, fast-food restaurants, and family restaurants often serve them. You can make them at home, too. They are a good food for lunch, supper, or a snack. They are nutritious. Can you name the food groups represented by each ingredient?

MENU 1

Mexican Tacos

Tacos

Preparing the Tacos

This is how you make eight tacos:

1. Gather the equipment. You'll need a baking pan, frying pan, wooden spoon, liquid measuring cup, paring knife, cutting board, potholders, and grater.
2. Gather the taco ingredients. You'll need 1 pound ground beef, 1 package taco seasoning, water, 2 small tomatoes, 8 lettuce leaves, ¼ pound cheddar cheese, and 8 taco shells.
3. Preheat the oven to 350° F.
4. Brown the meat in the frying pan. Then drain off the fat.
5. Stir in the taco seasoning mix and ¾ cup water.
6. Cook the meat sauce at a low heat for 15 minutes until the sauce is thick. Stir it occasionally with a wooden spoon.
7. Put the taco shells on a baking pan.
8. Place them in the preheated oven for 5 minutes.
9. Wash the lettuce and tomatoes, and drain.
10. Remove the stem from the tomatoes with the knife.
11. On the cutting board, chop the tomatoes into small pieces.
12. On the cutting board, slice the lettuce leaves into thin shreds.
13. Grate the cheese with the grater.
14. Using potholders remove the pan of heated taco shells from the oven. Turn off the oven.
15. Fill the taco shells with meat, then cheese, then tomatoes, and last shredded lettuce. Serve them while they're hot!

Cleaning Up and Evaluating the Tacos

Remember to clean up. You need to wash the equipment and counters carefully. Be sure to put everything away properly, too.

Next time you might make tacos with other toppings. These are some foods that taste good on tacos: sliced olives, sour cream, taco sauce, and chopped onions.

CHAPTER REVIEW

Summary

There are many different places to eat away from home. The school cafeteria serves nutritious, low-cost meals. Fast-food restaurants provide quick service, consistent quality food, and clean surroundings. Family restaurants are more leisurely. Fancy restaurants are more expensive and serve elaborately prepared food. Ethnic restaurants serve the special dishes of other countries and cultures.

The restaurant menu shows what foods are available. In family and fancy restaurants, a tip is left for service after the bill is paid.

Good manners are important when you eat out. In a restaurant, there are special rules to follow for the way you act.

What Have You Learned?

1. Why is a school lunch nutritious when you eat all five items served?
2. Why do people like fast-food restaurants?
3. How would you compare the food and service in a cafeteria, fast-food restaurant, and a family restaurant?
4. What is a gourmet restaurant?
5. Describe foods in three types of ethnic restaurants.
6. What are five rules for restaurant manners?
7. Why is a taco a nutritious food?

Things to Do

1. Name a restaurant you know that fits each category: fast-food restaurant, family restaurant, fancy restaurant, ethnic restaurant.
2. With another student demonstrate how to order, pay the bill, and tip.
3. Check the Yellow Pages in the phone book to find ethnic restaurants in your town. Write down the names of two of them.
4. Bring in to class menus from several restaurants. Write down the foods you might order for dinner. Include the cost of each food. Total the bill. What is an appropriate tip? How did you calculate it?

WORKING WITH FOODS

career	a lifetime occupation
cashier	someone who adds up the costs of purchases and takes in the money
caterer	someone other than the host or hostess whose job it is to prepare and often serve food for a special event
chef	the head cook, specially trained to prepare food in elaborate and precise ways
dietitian	a person with a college degree and special training in nutrition
employee	someone who works for someone else
employer	the boss
food service	any type of job that involves preparing food, serving food, or cleaning up after food is prepared and served
home economist	a person with a college degree in home economics
inventory	a record of the amount of items on hand

After reading this chapter, you should be able to:

- *list five important qualities for working with foods.*
- *describe five jobs in food service.*
- *identify three part-time food jobs for a high school student.*
- *describe three food jobs for a college graduate.*

"I got a job today!" For many people, it feels good to say they have a job.

What's so wonderful about working? It means different things to different people. Some reasons why people like to work are:

- to earn money for spending, savings, or helping the family live better.
- to give them the feeling of doing something worthwhile.
- to make them feel more adult like and responsible.
- to get the chance to meet and to work with other people.
- to gain experience.

275

Many high school students go to work at part-time jobs after school. Many of these jobs involve working with food.

There are many opportunities for jobs relating to foods. Many kinds of jobs match these reasons for working. In fact, the world of foods is very exciting! People who like to work with food can get a beginning job without having any previous training. Or they can become well trained and educated for more skilled work in higher paying jobs with food.

Preparing Yourself for a Job

Suppose you want a part-time job in food while you're in school or a full-time job later. What do you need to know? How must you act?

What you need to know about food and nutrition depends upon the job. Some jobs require a great deal of knowledge, even a college degree in food and nutrition. But for many jobs, people learn while they are working. Most food jobs for high school students give on-the-job training.

Employers look for certain qualities when they hire employees. An *employer* is the boss. An *employee* is someone who works for someone else. Employers usually want workers who are:

- healthy. You should be willing and able to work hard and often do physical work.
- clean. People who work with food need to take special care to have a clean body, clean hair, healthy teeth, and clean and neat clothing.
- trustworthy. You should be able to be trusted with other peoples' money, children, food, and belongings.
- cheerful and friendly. You want to be someone people like to work with and be with.
- reliable. You should get to work on time, follow directions, and do your share of the work.
- neat. Don't be messy. If you do accidentally make a mess, take care to thoroughly clean it up right away.
- considerate. You should help and respect others.
- able to speak clearly. You should be able to talk to others in a manner that can be easily understood.

Can you think of other things that would make you a good employee now? How about in the future? There are many things you can do now that can help make you a better employee when you're ready. School activities teach you to be a good worker and how to work with other people. You can learn about food at school, at home, and with friends.

Employers look for certain qualities in employees. When you go to an interview be on time, dress neatly, speak clearly, and be cheerful.

Jobs for High School Students

Most jobs for high school students require no experience or training. This lets you try different jobs working with food. Later, if you want a career in food, you'll have experience. You'll also be more likely to know what you want to do after you have tried different jobs. A *career* is a lifetime occupation, or type of work.

Supermarkets, fast-food restaurants, and family restaurants hire many high school students.

Jobs in Supermarkets

Many supermarkets hire students for part-time work. Supermarket jobs might include:

- helping customers find things in the store.
- receiving shipments and filling shelves.
- putting up shelf labels.
- packaging, weighing, and counting fresh foods such as apples, green beans, and nuts for customers.
- arranging displays at the ends of shelves and in windows.
- being a cashier at the check-out counter. A *cashier* adds up the purchases, takes the money, makes change, and may put the groceries in the bag.
- bagging food after it goes through the check-out counter.
- taking bags of food to cars and bringing in shopping carts.

After high school, people with experience might get a job in the office. They might cash checks and keep records.

Supermarkets offer a variety of part-time jobs for teenagers.

Jobs in Fast-Food Restaurants

With more and more fast-food restaurants, there are more and more part-time and summer jobs for high school students. Fast-food restaurant jobs might include:

- writing orders at the counter or a drive-up window.
- getting the order and putting it on a tray or in a bag.
- collecting money and making change.
- preparing food for a salad bar and keeping it filled and tidy.
- preparing and cooking foods, such as hamburgers, tacos, fried fish, fries, or coffee.
- taking inventory. *Inventory* is a record of the amount of items on hand.
- keeping the cooking, food storage, and serving areas clean.
- cleaning the dining area.

Some people start as part-time employees. Later, when they get out of high school, they get more training and become managers.

Fast food restaurants also offer a variety of part-time jobs.

Waiting tables in a restaurant is a popular part-time job.

Jobs in Family Restaurants

Family restaurants hire high school students, too. Like fast-food restaurants, this is a food service job. A *food service* job is any job which involves preparing or serving food for groups of people, or the cleaning up after the food is prepared and served.

In a family restaurant, a teenager might have one of these jobs:

- A waiter or waitress sets tables, takes orders, pours water, serves food, and writes the bill.
- A busperson clears tables, stacks dishes, and takes dirty dishes to the kitchen.
- A dishwasher cleans off trays and runs the large dishwashing machine.
- In the kitchen, there are many jobs in food preparation: kitchen helper, salad worker, sandwich maker, assistant baker, assistant cook, and beverage worker.

Food service jobs like these exist whether you live in a city, in a small town, or in the country. These are some other places you might look: hotel and motel restaurants, nursing homes, business cafeterias, hospitals, and schools.

Jobs after High School

After you finish high school, you can have any of the jobs already described, or you can get more training and experience. Trade schools can give one or two years of special training in food. Jobs which require more knowledge usually pay more and give more responsibility.

Jobs in Restaurants

High school students get beginning jobs in restaurants. But people who go to a trade school can learn jobs that require special skills. These are jobs they might learn to do: pastry cook, baker, meat cutter, cook, kitchen supervisor, storeroom supervisor, or dining room supervisor.

Some people also go to special schools to become chefs. A chef is the head cook. Chefs learn to carefully prepare food in fancy and elaborate ways.

Jobs in Catering Services

A catering service prepares food for a party, a picnic, a church or other meeting place, or even for a home. Sometimes food is prepared ahead, packaged, and delivered. The caterer doesn't stay. Other times, the caterer stays to finish preparing the food and to serve it. A *caterer* is someone other than the host or hostess who prepares and often serves food for a special event. Catering jobs might include:

- preparing foods. You might start as a helper. Then you might chop vegetables, shape meat patties, and measure ingredients. With experience, you could become a cook.
- packaging foods so they can be transported someplace else.
- packing dishes, glasses, flatware, and linens.
- delivering and serving food. You might set tables, wait on tables, or serve the food. Or you might serve each person at the serving table and keep the food dishes filled.
- assisting in cleaning up during and after the event.

Catering services do all the food preparation and service for you. You just have to pay! Many catering services hire part-time employees.

Other Food Service Jobs

Besides restaurants and catering, people specially trained in food service work in hospitals, child-care centers, schools, and businesses.

In a hospital, a food-service worker might also prepare trays for patients, help patients choose from the menu, feed patients who can't feed themselves, and prepare special snacks.

People who like working with children might prepare food at a child-care center. They might also feed toddlers, teach children good table manners, and take care of spills.

Schools and businesses usually serve cafeteria style. Cafeteria style food-service is fast. Responsibilities of jobs there might be:

- making a menu board.
- arranging counters with trays of food.
- filling the serving areas where food stays hot.
- putting food on plates as people go through the line.
- keeping the dining areas clean.

Jobs in Small Food Shops

Many shops, such as bakeries, sell food to customers to take home. As a high school student, you might assist in preparing food, or you might serve customers. With experience, you can prepare the food yourself. You might even want to own and operate your own food shop someday.

Some of the various duties of jobs in food shops include:

- arranging displays of food.
- preparing the food. This might include filling pie shells, slicing meat or bread, or making salads.
- waiting on customers, adding up bills, and making change.
- packaging the food orders.
- washing cooking utensils.
- washing out display areas.

Small bakeries hire part-time workers, too. They usually start by waiting on customers. With experience you can learn to prepare the food and even to manage the business.

Jobs in Food Processing Companies

Companies involved in the processing of foods are responsible for getting the food from the farmer to the food consumer. There are many full-time jobs in food processing where you can be trained on the job.

Convenience foods, which you learned about in chapter 8, are made by food processors. These are some businesses that process food:

- meat-packing plant
- vegetable or fruit cannery
- dairy company where milk is pasteurized and bottled, and where ice cream and yogurt are made
- cheese factory

The processing plant is like a kitchen, but it uses recipes or formulas for hundreds or thousands of people. If you worked there you might:

- be responsible for one step in the formula for preparing the food.
- care for the machines which put food in packages.
- get the finished products ready for delivery.

With experience, you could become a supervisor.

Here we see two processing plants. One is making ice cream cones. The other makes ice cream. In the photo below the large containers are being sealed for shipment to retail stores.

Jobs After College

For many of the top jobs in food, you need a college degree in food, nutrition, or restaurant administration. There are many exciting jobs you can prepare for.

Jobs in Teaching

Many teachers know a lot about food. They also know how to help people learn. Food and nutrition teachers have at least one college degree in home economics. People with a college degree in home economics are called *home economists*.

There are many opportunitites for people who want to teach about food. High schools, colleges, and adult education programs hire home economics teachers. There are also many cooking schools that need teachers.

A foods teacher must:

- know about food and nutrition.
- be able to speak clearly in front of a group.
- know how to teach.
- be well-organized.
- enjoy being with people.
- enjoy learning.

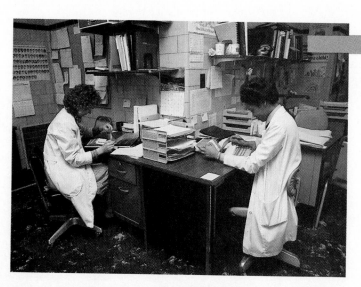

Dieticians are professionals with college degrees in nutrition who perform a variety of jobs in hospitals. Here you see two dieticians planning menus for patients based on the doctors' directions.

Jobs in Hospitals and Health Centers

Besides food service employees, hospitals and health centers hire people with advanced training in nutrition. These people are called *dietitians*. They have a college degree and one additional year of special training afterwards.

A dietitian can have many jobs in a hospital. Some dietitians are responsible for all the meals served to patients, hospital employees, and visitors. They plan menus, including special menus, for sick people. They supervise how food service employees order, store, prepare, and serve food. And they train workers, too. Some work requires a computer.

Dietitians talk with doctors and patients in hospitals and health centers. They plan menus for people who can't eat regular foods or who need to lose weight. Fitness programs provide new jobs for dietitians. In such programs, dietitians help healthy people plan menus that help them stay healthy!

Some hospitals employ people with two years of college education in nutrition to help the dietitian.

Jobs with Newspapers, Magazines, Television

Newspapers and magazines contain many stories about food and nutrition. Newspapers may have a whole section devoted to food. There are many magazines which deal only with food.

If you like to write, you might write food articles for a newspaper or magazine. As you learn more, you might become the food editor. The editor plans the food stories and the pictures.

People who write about food also work in advertising. For example, they write ads for television and magazines. Some of them write textbooks and even prepare films.

With training, a person with a strong background in food and nutrition may also appear on television and radio to discuss food and nutrition.

Jobs with Food Companies

Home economists and dietitians also work for food companies. Many times they have taken business courses in college, too. Examples of such jobs are:

- **consumer services.** Home economists and dietitians help companies know what consumers want and need. Part of their job may be to handle consumer complaints. They also tell consumers about the foods the company makes. This includes answering consumer letters. The government also hires home economists to tell consumers about food.
- **recipe and label writing.** Home economists develop recipes for their company's products. Then they write the information for the food labels.
- **food styling.** Home economists prepare food for photography. They know special ways to make food pictures in cookbooks and magazines look very appetizing and appealing. This is a good job for people who enjoy art as well as food.
- **booklet writing.** Home economists and dietitians write booklets about foods made by their company. They work with artists and printers. You may have used some of these booklets in class.
- **new food product development.** Companies create new food products for consumers. Some home economists may study consumer needs. Others might create the new food to meet those needs. This job requires considerable knowledge of science.
- **sales.** People with a strong background in food and nutrition and who enjoy meeting people often make good salespeople. They sell their products to supermarkets, bakeries, restaurants, hospitals, and other food service organizations. Then these places can sell the food to you.

Food jobs are exciting. If you enjoy food, a job or even a career in food might be right for you!

CHAPTER REVIEW

Summary

Wherever you live, there are a variety of jobs for people who want to work with food.

High school students can work in supermarkets, fast-food restaurants, and family restaurants. These jobs usually require no experience or training.

Many jobs after high school require experience or extra training. Some jobs provide on-the-job training. Others require more schooling.

Food service offers many jobs which might become a career. The top jobs usually require a college degree in food, nutrition, or restaurant administration.

What Have You Learned?

1. What is a career?
2. If you were being hired for a food job, what are five qualities an employer might look for?
3. Describe three jobs a high school student might apply for.
4. What are some duties of a fast-food restaurant employee?
5. What are some duties of a supermarket employee?
6. List five jobs in food service.
7. What are the advantages of getting more training and experience for a job in food service?
8. What is a home economist? A dietitian? A chef? What kind of education and experience must they have?

Things to Do

1. Interview someone with a job in food service. Find out what the person does and what they needed to know to get the job. Write a report about what you learn.
2. Bring in the "Want Ads" from a newspaper that tell about food jobs. Discuss them in class. Then make a bulletin board with the ads.
3. Ask the food service staff in your school to talk to the class about their jobs.

GLOSSARY

a la cart (ah la KART). When each food is ordered separately from the menu.

anorexia (a nor ECKS ee ah). An eating behavior in which people have such a fear of being fat that they severely starve themselves.

appetite (AP puh tyt). The desire to eat.

appetizer (AP puh ty zur). Food that starts a meal and is served before the main course.

appliances (uh PLY uhn suhz). Food preparation equipment that needs gas or electricity to operate. Some small appliances are blenders, toasters, and electric mixers. Large appliances include stoves, refrigerators, and dishwashers.

aroma (uh ROH muh). The way a food smells.

bake. To cook by dry heat in an oven.

balanced breakfast. Breakfast which provides about one-fourth of the day's nutrient needs with servings from the four main food groups in the Daily Food Guide.

balanced diet. Daily menus which meet the recommendations of the Daily Food Guide, providing the recommended servings from each of the four main food groups.

baste. To moisten with melted butter, cooking liquid, or other liquid while food roasts or bakes. The liquid is usually applied using a spoon, ladle, brush, or baster.

batter (BAT tur). Thin mixture of flour, liquid, and other liquids. When you mix a packaged cake mix with eggs, water, and oil you make a cake batter.

beat. To mix ingredients quickly until smooth, usually done with an electric mixer or a spoon.

blend. To mix two or more ingredients completely.

boil. To cook liquids at a high temperature where bubbles form, rise, and break.

braise (BRAYZ). To cook meat or poultry slowly in a small amount of liquid in a covered pan.

breakfast. Morning meal.

broil. To cook at a high temperature by direct heat. Cooking meat on a barbecue grill is an example of broiling.

broth (BRAHTH). Liquid left after cooking meat, poultry, or fish in water. Another name for stock. Broth is often used to make soup.

brunch. Meal served late in the morning which usually serves as both breakfast and lunch.

budget (BUHJ uht). A plan for the way you spend your money.

buffet (buh FAY) **style.** Way of serving food in which food is placed on the table in serving dishes and the guests help themselves, then carry their food somewhere else to eat.

bulimia (bu LEE mee uh). An eating disorder in which people overeat, then make themselves vomit to get rid of the food they just ate so they won't gain any weight.

calorie (KAL uh ree). A unit for measuring energy. The amount of energy food provides your body is measured in calories.

calorie chart. Chart which lists foods in certain size servings and tells the number of calories one serving provides.

carbohydrate (kar bo HY drate). Nutrient which provides energy and is found mostly in grain foods, fruits and vegetables, and foods made with sugar.

career (kuh REER). Lifetime occupation.

cashier (kash EER). Someone who adds up the costs of purchases and takes in the money for them.

casserole (KAS uh role). Combination of several ingredients baked and served in the same baking dish and often served as a one-dish meal. For example, tuna, noodles, peas, celery, and mushroom soup can be mixed and cooked together to make a casserole.

caterer (KAY ter er). Someone who is hired to provide, prepare, and often serve food for a special event.

centerpiece. An attractive decoration placed in the center of the table. A bouquet of flowers or a bowl of fruit makes a nice centerpiece.

chef (SHEF). The head cook in a restaurant who has been specially trained to prepare food in elaborate and precise ways.

chemical cold pack. Container of liquid which, when frozen, is colder than ice and stays cold longer than ice. It is used to help keep carried foods cold.

chop. To cut into small pieces with a knife or other cutting utensil.

citrus fruit. Fruit such as oranges, grapefruit, and tangerines. Citrus fruit is a good source of vitamin C.

combination foods. Foods that belong in two or more food groups. Pizza and tacos are two examples.

comparison shopping. Comparing items to get the best buy for your money. To comparison shop for foods, compare the cost, nutrients, ingredients, size or amount, and freshness of similar foods to choose the best buy.

condensed (kuh DENST) **soup.** Convenience soup which has had some water removed when it was made, so you must add liquid when preparing it. Canned tomato soup is an example.

consumer (kuh SOO mer). Person who buys and uses certain items, such as food.

convenience foods. Foods that help save you time because they have already been partly prepared when you buy them. Cake mixes, refrigerated cookie dough, and frozen pizza are convenience foods.

convenience store. Store which handles just the basic grocery items, but is usually handy, quick to get in and out of, and usually open when other stores may be closed.

converted (kuh VER tuhd) **rice.** Rice that is partly cooked, then dried, and packaged to sell in stores.

coupon (KOO pon). A certificate that offers cents off the price of certain foods.

course. All the foods that are served at one time. These are the courses on many menus: appetizer, soup, salad, entree, and dessert.

cuts of meat. Large sections of meat are cut from the animal, and these are then cut into smaller pieces of meat called "cuts" which we buy in the store. The names of these cuts often refer to the part of the animal the meat came from, such as the shoulder cut and the rib cut.

daily food guide. Guideline for planning and judging a balanced diet.

dash. Very small amount of an ingredient. It's less than $\frac{1}{8}$ teaspoon.

deep-fat fry. To cook in hot fat or oil that is deep enough for the food to float in.

dehydrated soup. Convenience dry soup. It has all the water removed, so you must add liquid before heating it.

dessert (dee ZURT). Last course of a meal. Examples of dessert are fruit, cookies, cake, and ice cream.

dice. To cut into very small pieces.

diet (DY uht). All the foods people eat and drink.

dietitian (DY uh tih shuhn). A person with a college degree and special training in nutrition. A dietitian plans special nutritious menus and often supervises how the food is handled, prepared, and served.

digestion (dy JEHS chuhn). Body process of breaking down food into nutrients the body can use.

dinner. Biggest meal of the day. Can be eaten midday or in the evening.

dovetail. To do more than one task at a time. For example, you can make the best use of your time, or dovetail your work, if you prepare the salad for a meal while a chicken is baking.

drain. To remove liquid from food by pouring off the liquid, by placing the food in a utensil with holes, or by placing the food on paper towels to absorb the liquid.

dressing. Sauce added to salads to add flavor.

dry heat. Cooking with no liquids, such as broiling and baking.

emotions (ee MOH shuhnz). The way you feel about things. Anger, joy, fear, and sadness are all examples of emotions.

employee (ehm ploy EE). Someone who works for someone else.

employer (ehm PLOY er). The boss.

empty-calorie foods. Foods which provide calories but few nutrients. These foods are usually high in carbohydrate or fat. Soda, butter, and jelly are examples.

enriched (en RICHT) **cereals.** Refined cereals with vitamins and minerals added.

entertaining. Having a party or inviting someone home.

entree (AHN tray). Main course of a meal.

ethnic (EHTH nik) **foods.** Foods from people who come from various parts of the world. Tacos, lasagna, and egg rolls are examples of ethnic foods.

evaluate (ee VAL yoo ayt). To judge something. When you prepare a meal you can evaluate it by asking yourself if everything turned out right, identifying any problems you may have had, and finding ways you can do better next time.

fad diet. A diet for losing weight that is very popular only for a short time.

family style. Way of serving meals in which all the food for several people is placed on the table in serving dishes. The dishes of food are passed around the table and the people sitting at the table help themselves.

fast foods. Foods prepared and served fast in a restaurant where you order and are served at a counter.

fat. A nutrient which gives energy. It is an oily substance found in most animal products and some plants. Butter and vegetable oil are mostly fat. Peanut butter, meat, and cheese have some fat along with many other nutrients.

fiber (FY bur). A non-digestible carbohydrate that helps move food through your body during digestion. Good sources of fiber are whole-grain breads and cereals, fruits, vegetables, and nuts.

flatware. Eating utensils—knives, forks, and spoons.

flour. To cover lightly with flour.

food groups. Foods are divided into five food groups according to the nutrients they contain. The four main food groups are the Milk and Cheese Group, the Fruit and Vegetable Group, the Bread and Cereal Group, and the Meat, Poultry, Fish, and Beans Group. The fifth group is the Fats and Sweets Group which provides calories but few nutrients.

food habits. The types of foods you eat, when you eat, and how you eat.

food service. Any type of job that involves preparing or serving food, or cleaning up after food is served and prepared. Food service jobs include cooks, waitresses, caterers, and buspersons.

foods lab. Kitchen in the classroom.

frosting. Cake topping.

fruit drink. Beverage which only has a small amount of real fruit juice. The rest is sugar, water, added flavorings, and often vitamin C.

fruit juice. Beverage which is 100% real fruit juice, with no water added.

frying. Cooking in fat or oil.

garnish (GAHR nihsh). A food used to decorate another food.

germs. Living things which are too small to see with the eye alone, but which can spread illness. When preparing food you must make sure you, the work place, and the food are all clean so germs cannot grow on the food.

gourmet (goor MAY) **restaurants.** Fancy restaurants which offer elaborately prepared meals often in elegant surroundings.

grate. To rub food on the rough surface of a grater to make small pieces.

grease. To rub with fat or oil. To grease a pan, you use a paper towel or piece of wax paper to rub fat or oil all over the inside of the pan, including the corners.

hard-cooked eggs. Eggs still in the shell which are simmered until both the yolks and the whites are firm.

home economist (HOHM ee KON ah mist). A person with a college degree in home economics.

host. Boy or man who entertains guests.

hostess. Girl or woman who entertains guests.

household energy. Gas or electricity needed to power household appliances and to provide light and heat.

impulse buying. Buying something you didn't plan to because it looks or smells good, because it's new, or because you "just felt like it."

ingredients (ihn GREED ee uhntz). Specific foods that are part of a recipe. Cheese and sausage are two ingredients in a pizza.

ingredient list. Information on a food label which lists the ingredients in order by weight. The ingredient that is present in the greatest amount is listed first, and the ingredient used in the least amount is listed last.

instant rice. Boxed convenience form of rice that has been cooked and then dried before packaging.

insulated container. Container which helps keep hot foods hot or cold foods cold. ice chests and vacuum bottles are examples.

inventory (IN vuhn tor ee). The amount of things you have on hand.

invitation. Asking someone to come as a guest.

leftovers. Foods left from a previous meal.

level off. To fill a measuring utensil as full as possible with a dry ingredient and then use a spatula or knife to scrape across the top of the contents to make sure the measuring cup or spoon is completely full, but not over-filled.

lifestyle. The way you live.

manage. To use your resources wisely.

mash. To make a food soft and smooth by beating or crushing.

measure. To find out the amount of something.

melt. To change a solid to a liquid, using heat.

menu (MEHN yoo). A list of foods to be served at a meal.

microwave cooking. Fast way to cook using a microwave oven.

minerals (MIHN uh ruhlz). Nutrients that become part of the bones, teeth, and blood and that are used by the body in its many processes. Iron and calcium are two important minerals.

moist heat. Cooking in liquid, such as braising or stewing.

nutrient label. Information on a food label that tells what nutrients the food contains and the amount of each nutrient one serving will provide.

nutrients (NOO tree uhntz). Substances in food which your body uses to keep you well, give you energy, and help you grow.

nutrition (noo TRIHSH uhn). The study of nutrients in the food you eat and the way your body uses them.

nutritious (noo TRIHSH uhs). Description of foods which provide you with many important nutrients.

one-dish meal. Meal cooked and often served in one cooking utensil. The main ingredient is usually a protein food such as meat or chicken. It also usually includes at least one vegetable and a food high in carbohydrate, such as rice or pasta.

pan fry. To cook in a small amount of fat or oil.

party mix. Mixture of nuts, seeds, and other dry snack foods served as a party snack.

pasta (PAHS tuh). Food made with flour and water. Spaghetti, macaroni, and noodles are all forms of pasta.

pasteurize (PASS tyoor ize). To heat fresh milk to a certain temperature for a long enough time to destroy any harmful germs it might contain.

peel. To remove the skin from food.

pinch test. Way to estimate body weight by pinching together the skin of certain areas of your body and measuring the thickness of the fold of skin you have pinched.

place setting. Table arrangement of dishes, glasses, flatware, and napkin for one person at a meal.

poultry (POHL tree). Chicken, turkey, or other birds sold as food.

preheat. To heat the oven to the temperature you need before using it for cooking.

pre-preparation. Any task that can be done ahead of other steps in a recipe. When making pizza, you can pre-prepare by grating the cheese and keeping it in a container in the refrigerator until you are ready to put it on the pizza.

produce (PROH doos). Fresh fruits and vegetables.

protein. Nutrient that helps your body grow and repair itself. Some good sources of protein are beef, chicken, eggs, and peanut butter.

punch. Beverage made by mixing several kinds of beverages, such as a combination of two or more fruit juices.

quick breads. Light, airy breads made from batter or dough which rises as it cooks. Examples are pancakes, muffins, and most biscuits.

rain check. A certificate that lets you buy an item at the sale price in the future if the store runs out of the item during the sale.

receipt (rih SEET). Cash register slip which acts as a record of your purchase.

reception (ree SEP shun). Type of party, usually given to welcome someone.

recipe (REH sih pee). A set of food preparation instructions. A recipe tells you what ingredients you will need, how much of each ingredient is used, how the ingredients are combined, and, if needed, how to cook the combined ingredients.

refined cereal. Cereal made from grain after the outer layer of the grain seed or kernal has been removed.

refreshments. Food and beverage served at a party.

regional (REEJ uhn uhl) **foods.** Foods that have become special favorites in a particular part of the country. Examples of regional foods are New England's clam chowder and the South's pecan pie.

reservation (reh sur VAY shun). Place held or saved for you, usually at a restaurant.

resource (REE sors). Anything that you have that can help you accomplish what you want to do. Time, money, and your personal energy are important resources that you can use to accomplish what you want.

roast. To cook uncovered in an oven without liquid.

RSVP. To let the host or hostess know whether you will be able to attend his or her party or gathering.

salad. Mixture of two or more foods, most often made with different types of vegetables or fruit.

sandwich. Two or more slices of bread with food placed between them.

sandwich spread. Food spread on bread to keep it moist. Mayonnaise, margarine, and mustard can be used as sandwich spreads.

sauce (SAWSS). A liquid mixture used to flavor foods. Tomato sauce and barbecue sauce are two examples.

saute (saw TAY). To fry lightly and quickly in a small amount of fat.

schedule (SKEH dyool). A plan for how you will spend your time.

scrambled eggs. Eggs in which the whites and yolks are stirred together and then cooked in a little hot fat.

season. To add spices or herbs to change the flavor of food.

seasoning. Spices and herbs used to add flavor to a food. Salt, pepper, paprika, dill, and sage are examples of seasonings.

sherbet (SHUHR buht). Frozen dessert similar to ice cream, but contains more sugar and less fat than ice cream. Often has fruit or fruit juice for flavoring.

simmer (SIHM uhr). To cook in liquid just below the boiling point. Water is simmering when bubbles appear only along the edges of the pan.

snacks. Foods eaten between meals.

soup. A food made primarily with liquid. Often vegetables, meat, and/or pasta are added to the liquid to make a hearty meal.

speciality stores. Stores that specialize in one type of food, such as an ethnic food.

spoiled food. Food which is no longer safe to eat because disease-carrying germs have been allowed to grow on it.

steam. To cook, covered, over (not in) boiling water.

stew. To simmer food covered with liquid.

stir. To use a spoon to mix slowly in a circular motion.

stir-fry. To cook thinly-sliced food quickly in a small amount of fat. Many Oriental foods are prepared by stir-frying.

stock. Liquid left after cooking meat, poultry, or fish in water. Stock is often used to make soup.

strain. To remove liquid from food using a utensil that has holes.

taco (TAH koh). Fried tortilla, folded and filled with meat, tomatoes, cheese, and lettuce.

taste buds. Parts of the tongue that identify different tastes.

texture (TEHKS chuhr). The way food feels when you eat it. When you eat a carrot, it has a crunchy texture. Mashed potatoes feel smooth as you eat them.

thaw. To bring something frozen to room temperature.

theme party. Specific idea on which a party is based. If the theme of a party is a holiday, then the food, decorations, and games will all be related to that holiday.

tip. Money you pay a waiter or waitress for service.

tortilla (tor TEE yuh). Round, flat bread made from corn or wheat. It is often used to make other Mexican foods, such as tacos and burritos.

tossed salad. Salad made with lettuce, and perhaps other greens, plus sliced or chopped vegetables such as tomatoes, carrots, and celery.

unit price. Price of a food per ounce, pound, or quart. For example, if a 48-ounce can of tomato juice costs $1.20, the unit price is 2.5 cents per ounce.

utensils (yoo TEN silz). Kitchen tools and equipment used for preparing and serving food. Some examples of utensils are paring knives, rolling pins, frying pans, and cooling racks.

vegetarian (vehj uh TEHR ee uhn). Person who does not eat meat, poultry, or fish.

vitamins. Nutrients that help direct the way other nutrients and your body work.

wax paper. Paper with a coating of wax to protect it from moisture.

weight control. Achieving or keeping your own best body weight through proper diet and exercise.

wellness. Being totally healthy in mind, body, and emotions.

whip. To mix or beat very fast in order to add air and volume to a mixture.

whole-grain cereal. Cereal made from the entire kernel or seed of grain.

wok. A special kind of frying pan used in stir-frying. It is wide at the top and narrow at the bottom.

yeast (YEEST). Ingredient used to make dough rise.

CREDITS

Bill Atherton, 12, 14, 24, 28, 41, 66, 104, 108, 116, 128, 146, 202, 221, 236, 248, 254, 281

Campbell Soup, 210

Dairy Council, Inc. Dairy Council of Central States, Inc., St. Louis District Dairy Council, 261

Howard Davis, 89, 90, 91, 92, 94, 215

James B. Gaffney, 219, 224, 264

Impact Communications/Wendy Boersema & Paul Walker, 10-11, 15, 20, 21, 22, 28, 33, 36, 40, 43, 46-47, 48, 49, 50, 51, 52, 53, 55, 57, 58, 60, 64-65, 66, 67, 84, 85, 87, 88, 95, 96, 105, 107, 109, 111, 113, 115, 117, 122, 123, 127, 129, 130, 132, 134, 136-137, 138, 140, 141, 143, 144, 145, 147, 148, 152, 155, 159, 160, 162, 163, 166, 168-169, 170, 171, 172, 173, 175, 176, 177, 180, 182, 184-185, 188, 189, 190, 193, 195, 196, 198, 201, 204-205, 206, 207, 208, 210, 212, 213, 214, 217, 224, 225, 226, 230-231, 232, 233, 235, 238, 241, 244-245, 247, 249, 251, 252, 253, 256, 260, 266, 268, 271, 274-275, 277, 279

Mike Jenkins, 73, 263, 271, 279, 280, 283, 284

Morraine Valley Community College, 276

National Live Stock & Meat Board, 207, 210

The Pantagraph, 18

Liz Purcell, 13, 30 ,70, 154, 174, 218

St. Francis Medical Center, Peoria, IL, 286

Sandra Savage, 125

William Seabright, 26-27, 82-83, 102-103, 120-121, 150-151, 258-259

Slater Assoc./Image Gate, 98, 175, 211

Courtesy of Taco Bell Corp., 39, 263

Texas Highways, 285

Texas Pecan Growers Assn., Inc., 19

United Dairy Industry, 237

Alice Vernon, Food Stylist, 15, 52, 55, 57, 58, 64-65, 66, 122, 123, 129, 155, 184-185, 189, 238, 266

Wendy's International, Inc., 263

Whirlpool Corporation, 37

Duane Zehr, 77, 157, 251

INDEX

Thyroid gland, 213
Timing the meal, 146
Togetherness and food, 15
Tomato-Cheese Soup,
    preparation, 182
Tortilla, 27
Trade schools, 282
Trail Mix recipe, 99
Training on the job, 276
Tuna Noodle Casserole,
    preparation, 197

U

Unit prices
    with package price, 252
    shelf label, 252
    utensils. See Kitchen
        stencils

V

Vegetable and Fruit Group,
    124, 155
Vegetables
    buying, 214
    from each plant part, 215
    (chart)
Vitamins, definition, 26, 32
    Vitamin A, 34, 155
    Vitamin B, 34
    Vitamin C, 45, 132, 156

W

Water
    in breakfast beverage, 151
    need for, 35
    as regulator, 35

Weight
    control, 155
    estimation, 61
    and exercise, 41
    menu planning, 80
Wellness. See also Health
    definition, 10
    and dietitians, 287
    and food, 12
    prevention of illness, 28
Washing dishes, 108